# THE METHOD OF SELLING

Your Key To Successful Sales with Over
70 Creative Selling Techniques

## Mark Benedict

CCB Publishing
British Columbia, Canada

The Method of Selling: Your Key to Successful Sales with Over 70
Creative Selling Techniques

Copyright © 2007 by Mark Benedict
ISBN-10: 0-9781162-5-9
ISBN-13: 978-0-9781162-5-5
First Edition

Library and Archives Canada Cataloguing in Publication
Benedict, Mark, 1975-
The method of selling: your key to successful sales with over 70 creative selling
techniques/ by Mark Benedict; foreword by David Straker.
Includes index.
Also available in electronic format.
ISBN 978-0-9781162-5-5
1. Selling.  I. Title.
HF5438.25.B447 2007   658.85   C2007-903659-7

Publisher:      CCB Publishing
                British Columbia, Canada
                www.ccbpublishing.com

# DEDICATION

I'd like to thank God for giving me the strength and wisdom to accomplish the task of writing a book that would not exist without his guidance and will. To Him I owe much thanks!!!

I'd also like to thank my mother, Juanita, whose sense of humor is reflected as well as documented in my style of writing. And my father, Foster – whose intensity always sparks a light wherever he goes – he sparked a light in every word I have ever thought.


Mark Benedict

# ACKNOWLEDGEMENTS

Thanks to my editor and publisher, Paul Rabinovitch, whose wisdom and advice have kept me on the straight and narrow path to successful writing and marketing. Indeed, failure is not an option.

And there are others to thank, whose names are too vast to mention and whose indirect and invisible works have cast a visible impression on me and all I do. To all of you, much thanks!

Mark Benedict

# FOREWORD

Sales is a very honest profession: either you sell something or you do not. There is little room for talking through your hat and crossing your fingers, as the evidence of your actions will be discovered very quickly. This makes for sales people who either keep learning and improving or who go and do something else. It also explains the many, many sales books out there. A number of these books are based on 'my success' and give an interesting view from the position of a single salesperson, although the value of these depends on the reader working in a similar position. Other books focus on a limited part of selling, from prospecting to closing. Only a few books cover the full spectrum. *The Method of Selling* is one of these. It is a complete book providing useful detail on the whole soup-to-nuts selling process.

My work on the changingminds.org web site is based on many years of experience and study in how one person changes the mind of another, and there is no profession more dedicated to this aim than sales. In selling you have to be a psychologist, a negotiator, a leader, a diplomat and many more things, as well as a product expert. *The Method of Selling* will help in all of these.

What Mark Benedict has done here is to combine learning from many different areas, from traditional sales wisdom to psychology and the nuances of modern Neuro-Linguistic Programming or NLP. Thus in these pages you will learn everything from a wide range of closing techniques to subtle methods of language and action that will lead your prospective customers to like you as a person and hence willingly move towards that wonderful close. Mark also delves into the psychology of the self – great sales people are positive people who like themselves as well as their customers.

*The Method of Selling* is, in brief, the most comprehensive book on selling I have had the pleasure to read for a long time. In the pages Mark Benedict has condensed an enormous amount of sales wisdom into a complete book on selling. So well done to you for buying it and now all you have to do is read it, digest it and become the success you know you can now be!

David Straker
changingminds.org

# TABLE OF CONTENTS

**TOPICS**                                                                       **PAGES**

# INTRODUCTION

In your hand is the answer to what makes all salespeople successful people. In your palm lays the method that the most accomplished salespeople in the world use to achieve wealth.

If you were to ask me to choose the most important topic in this book to succeed in sales, then I would say that sales is a combination of many ingredients that blend together to make it a successful process, like the ingredients that one uses to make a cake. But then again I would say that the most important ingredient to make a cake would not be one of the ingredients in the cake, but the ingredient of *desire* to first of all want to make the cake. So I would have to say that the most important ingredient of all to make a cake is the desire and willpower to make the cake. In that same manner, I would have to say that the most important topics in this book for someone who desires to be successful in sales are the topics about *believing in yourself*, so that you can be successful in sales.

If you have the willpower to make a cake, then you will automatically find the ingredients to make that cake. If you have the desire to be successful in sales, then you will automatically do everything you can to get the necessary tools needed to be successful in sales. It all starts with a desire and the willpower to achieve. And so shall it happen as you will and wish.

Reading this book means that you have a desire to be successful in sales. But the question is, "How strong is your desire?" Will your desire last when the storms of sales trouble come your way, and will you stand firm in the face of opposition? So now that you have the desire, all you need is to strengthen that desire to withstand the obstacles that sales has in store for you. Don't be afraid. Be courageous and strong. Your desire goes before you, and your willpower will strengthen you.

This book will *start* you off with more than enough tools that are necessary to be a successful salesperson and for you to enjoy the life of a successful sales living. All you have to do is provide the time and effort, and your story will be a successful one, hammered in the pages of all those who have gone before you and shall come after you in the great big book of successful salespeople.

This book answers many questions that you would expect to find in a sales book. After you have studied "the method" you should feel as one who can sell anything. And the feeling that you can accomplish something proclaims the fact that you can do it.

But this book not only teaches you how to be a successful salesperson, this book reveals to you that you already are a salesperson. Everybody is a salesperson. If you have ever persuaded anyone to do something, then it means that you are a salesperson. This book only strives to enhance you as a salesperson – to sharpen the blades of your sales might; to guide you on the road to a professional sales guru; to stamp your name with approval in the dean's list of sales. By studying this book, you have already attained your first stamp of approval.

# Topic 1

## KNOW WHAT YOU'RE REALLY SELLING

Sometimes we salespeople get off track of what we are really doing for OUR prospects who we are catering to. The following list gives you a real sense of what the prospect's reasons toward buying are:

| YOU'RE NOT SELLING | | YOU'RE REALLY OFFERING |
|---|---|---|
| Products & Services | _____ | Yourself |
| Houses | _____ | A Homely Connection |
| Vehicles/Cars | _____ | Home on Wheels: Safety, Reliability, Comfort, Speed, Economy, Room, Style |
| Cable TV Services | _____ | Home Entertainment Services |
| Food | _____ | Mouth Watering Delight |
| Books | _____ | Stimulation for the Mind |
| Clothing | _____ | Self-Expression |
| Pets | _____ | Companionship |
| Satellite Dish Services | _____ | Home Entertainments Services |
| Medical Equipments | _____ | Safety Systems for Healthy Living |
| Movie Tickets | _____ | The Opportunity to Sit Next to a Date |
| Cameras | _____ | Memories to Cherish Forever |

| | | |
|---|---|---|
| Boats | _____ | Smooth Getaway Experience from Land |
| Vacation Spots | _____ | A Moment in Paradise |
| Jewelry | _____ | Things that Make Us Feel More Special |
| Carpets | _____ | Soft Fabric for the Eyes and Feet |
| Vacuum Cleaners | _____ | Dust-Free Homes |
| Land Property | _____ | A Piece of the Pie |
| Security Alarms | _____ | 24 Hour Eye Alert from Intruders |
| Advertisement | _____ | More Customer Business |
| Air Filter System | _____ | Better Health / Youthful Appearance/Longer Lifespan |

❖

Changing your perception of what you are selling and personalizing it reminds you of the reason why people will love you and your product or service.

# Topic 2

## EVERYBODY IS A SALESPERSON

*It is what we think we know that keeps us from learning.*
  *- Chester Barnard*

*Everyone lives by selling something.*
  *- Robert Louis Stevenson*

What is selling? Selling is persuading. We sell ourselves all the time – it's not just pro sellers who sell. We sell ourselves when we go on a job interview, when we ask for or are on a date, when we need a favor or a request done, when we are giving advice to anyone, when we are voicing our viewpoints and beliefs, when we are trying to comfort someone, when we are arguing with someone, when we are rationalizing ideas within our own minds, when we are apologizing to others for our mistakes, when we are performing tasks on our jobs – some of which may seemingly have nothing to do with Sales, and yet indeed they do. All jobs are connected to Sales because our jobs are always to prove/convince/persuade someone or ourselves of our abilities. So yes, it's inescapable – everybody is a salesperson. Selling is persuading others that we are the one who they must feel confident dealing with!

Even babies are salespeople. They cannot talk but still they manage to use their body language and persuasive sounds to get what they want. And they are very persistent too. They will cry all day long until you give in to their demands, even if we don't know what those demands are.

Everything that's yours in your house is there because either someone sold something to you or you sold it to yourself. Yes, we even sell ourselves.

You can't hide from it. Sales is what makes the world go round.

They say that prostitution is the oldest profession. Wrong! Selling is the oldest profession. Before they chose that profession they had to sell themselves on the idea that they were going to be who they are; and they had to sell that trade if they wanted to receive a profit. The president of your company is a salesperson. Doctors and nurses are salespeople. Mechanics know they are salespeople. Your local banker is a salesperson. Everybody is a salesperson. However some of us just don't realize it.

Not only are people everywhere salespeople, but also things and ideas are sale-things and sales-ideas. Your television is a sales-thing, trying to sell you stuff twenty-four hours a day. Your bed is a sales-thing, trying to sell you reasons to sleep on it – bragging about itself being soft and smooth. But is it really? The idea of, "Give me liberty or give me death" is a sales-pitch in itself, regardless of Patrick Henry's original intent back in 1775.

You can't escape it – selling is within you and all of us. The sun is selling us all its great features and benefits as it shines upon us and gives us warmth from the cold days ahead.

Selling is not a strange and dirty profession. We all do it all the time and will continue to do it until the end of time. Sales is what makes the world go round.

Sales is not just about a bunch of car salesmen trying to nickel and dime every penny out of you. Stop giving Sales a limited name. Sales sits in the most respected parts of society. But Sales does not discriminate, it will meet whoever wants to bargain in the gutters of life. Stand up and be proud of the oldest profession in the world. You are the salesperson of the year, and you're proud of it. Why? Sales is the fiber of life.

# Topic 3

---

## THE FOUR MAIN REASONS WHY PROSPECTS WILL BUY FROM YOU

*The golden rule for every business man is this: Put yourself in your customer's place.*
  *- Orison Swett Marden*

Most prospects who buy are going to buy based on one of the reasons listed below. This should give you a clearer picture of what and where you should be focusing on in order to turn on your prospects' buy mode.

1.  ***The first reason why a prospect will buy from you is simply because they like you.***

### WHAT WOULD MAKE A PERSON LIKE YOU:
  a.    Complimenting them, and/or finding common ground with them.
  b.    Your non-verbal form of communication, particularly your warm body language.

2.  ***The second reason why a prospect will buy from you is simply because they trust you.***

### WHAT WOULD MAKE A PERSON TRUST YOU:
  a.    Your non-verbal form of communication, particularly your warm body language will let them know that you are a trustworthy person.
  b.    What you say, including the way you say what you say will also communicate that you may be trusted because of your ethics and morals.

3.  *The third reason why a prospect will buy from you is because of price.* If by switching to your service(s) they will be saving money or if your offer is a great bargain, it's only logical for them to make the move that would be more profitable for them. This is why your opening statement of your product should, if possible, almost always include the possibility of saving money.

4.  *The fourth reason why a prospect will buy from you is because of quality/value.* If the product is better than the competition, more reliable, or more economical, or faster, then this would be more important than price for those who can afford it. Sometimes quality is more important to the prospect than price. Value is priceless!

## WHAT MAKES PROSPECTS BUY IN GENERAL?
*The first reason why people buy in general is because of want.*
Often times we hear salespeople say, "Change the customer's want into a need." In truth, that may be essential, but you can also change a prospective buyer's want into a buy without changing that want into a need. Often times for prospects a want can be stronger than a need. Therefore it is best to change a prospect's want into a desire – a must have.

*The second reason why people buy in general is because of need.*
*Need* is limited whereas *want* is infinite! Our human instinct is to want more than it needs. The bottom line is, if someone needs something, they're going to try to get it anyway. The question is, "Who are they going to get it from – you, or someone else?"

## WHY WOULD A PROSPECT WANT SOMETHING THEY DON'T NEED?
A prospect could want something they don't need for numerous reasons – the main ones being STATURE and PLEASURE. They like the way it

makes them look or feel. Pleasure is synonymous to want. Everyone wants pleasure even though they don't need it as an essential to survival.

Why Stature?: They like the way it makes them look.
Why Pleasure?: They like the way it makes them feel.

Pleasure could also include all the other senses: they like the way it looks, smells, tastes or sounds.

## BOTTOMLINE: CREATE A DESIRE FOR YOUR PRODUCT
Change the prospect's wants or needs, or lack of wants or needs into a must have now. Give them a good reason to desire what they once had no desire for. Bundle up their Sales experience into a DESIRE to obtain, and to obtain now, regardless of whether or not they initially wanted or needed your offer. Desire can be stronger than reasoning.

# Topic 4

---

## THE NUMBER ONE REASON WHY PROSPECTS WILL BUY FROM YOU

*I am a part of all that I have met.*
*- Alfred, Lord Tennyson*

The number one reason why a prospect will buy from you is for the mere fact that they like you. A prospect WILL like you if they think that both of you have something in common. The question is: "How do you show them that both of you have something in common?" It is not as difficult as you may think. Actually, it may be quite easy to achieve.

Firstly, the easiest way to show someone that both of you have something in common is to find something to compliment them on. The main point is to find something that seems sincere and that is actually a real compliment. For example: "I love those plants in front of your house, Jill. Did you plant them yourself? Where did you get them? I would love to have some of those!"

The second way to show a prospect that both of you have something in common is to pace them. Pacing a prospect is in essence mirroring and matching their natural behavior. It is *becoming like* them. It is *acting like* them. It is *behaving like* them. You may pace a prospect by:

✓ The words they use
✓ The speed at which they speak
✓ Their tone of voice
✓ Their body gestures
✓ Their body posture
✓ Their breathing rhythm
✓ The rate at which they blink
✓ Their emotional well-being

8

(Note: Do not try to mirror your prospect's body gestures immediately; instead, pause between four to twenty seconds before actually attempting it.)

The most difficult of acts to match with the prospect may be that of their breathing rhythm. Yet it has been observed, for example in yoga, that if everyone is matching each other's breathing rhythm in a room, then it creates a more relaxed state of well being for everyone.

Pacing a prospect's breathing rhythm may take more practice to master than any other. How do you know when someone is breathing in or out? When someone is inhaling (breathing in), their stomach "lifts" up a little bit. When they are exhaling (breathing out), their stomach relaxes in a slight downward motion.

**Important note**: Pacing someone does not mean mimicking or mocking them. Be careful not to come across this way. In fact, try not to come across in any one particular way to the prospect. They should not consciously detect you even pacing them.

The third way to show a prospect that both of you have something in common is to know how to use your own body language to put them at ease. Just be yourself and relaxed. The more relaxed you are or the more relaxed you appear in general, the more the prospect will trust you. And trust is just a by-product of their like for you. *Relax yourself* is the key phrase in having and showing good body language. You should maintain a relaxed body language even before coming in contact with the prospect. In fact, you should practice relaxing yourself in general, for this is the best way to seem approachable to ALL people.

The fourth way to show a prospect that both of you have something in common is to actually find a common ground that both of you share. If the prospect likes something like a certain food, clothing, sports game or any other hobby or activity or thing, find it, and talk about it. Share your thoughts about it with them. Ask them questions about it. Get yourself and them all excited about that common ground that both of you share, and they will love you!

Getting prospects to like you is not a hard thing – it's a human thing.

# Topic 5

## THE GREATEST CHALLENGE OF PERSUASION

*Doubt whom you will, but never yourself.*
  *- Christian Bovee*

Before you can convince or persuade anyone into buying anything from you, you must first be able to convince yourself of your own abilities. In other words, you must first *BUY* the idea that you can do it.

Use the present tense phrase, "I am…" or "I'm…" to achieve ANY goal. Make sure you're always using it in the present tense, as if you've already achieved it. Even more powerful than saying, "I will…" or "I can…" or "I shall…" say that you are it already. "I'm good at it," as in RIGHT NOW and NOT later.

Say to yourself: "I'm good at selling." Say this to yourself all the time, even if you don't believe it. Say it until your subconscious mind believes it. Keep on saying it: "I'm good at selling!" If you're disciplined enough to keep on thinking it and saying it, then it will indeed become a reality for you. In fact, the more you say it, the more you will automatically believe and become it.

What is the best way to learn how to persuade others? You do this by first learning how to persuade yourself. If you can persuade yourself that you are good at what you do, you will automatically persuade others about what you're good at doing!

Your toughest customer is YOURSELF. Once you have conquered yourself, you can conquer ANYTHING or ANYONE!

Use a phrase such as "I'm good at..." to guide you in convincing yourself that you are good at what you do. Examples:

I'm good at convincing.
I'm good at persuading.
I'm good at talking.
I'm good at lovemaking.
I'm good at telling jokes.
I'm good at selling.
I'm good at getting attention.
I'm good at learning.
I'm good at improvising.
I'm good at flirting.
I'm good at listening.
I'm good at getting what I want.
I'm good at attracting women.
I'm good at attracting men.
I'm good at being patient.
I'm good at explaining.
I'm good at telling stories.
I'm good at swimming.
I'm getting better at it.
I'm a morning person.
I like meeting new people.

I'm patient.
I'm a responsible person.
I'm going to sell TODAY!
I'm lucky!
I feel lucky!
I am lucky!
I'm feeling better.
I'm beginning to feel much
   better!
I'm feeling good.
I'm feeling relaxed.
I'm feeling optimistic.
I'm happy!
I'm feeling refreshed!
I'm feeling excited!
I'm feeling confident!
I know I can do it!
I am going to do it!
I am powerful!
I am power!

THESE ARE SUPER SENTENCES. YOU WILL RULE YOUR WORLD IF YOU THINK, SAY AND BELIEVE IN THEM!

Whatever you wish to be, say that you are it RIGHT NOW. Say or think, "I'm good at selling" TWO HUNDRED times each day without counting, for ten days straight. Then keep on maintaining your mind by saying or thinking it as often as you can. If you keep on thinking a certain way or saying a certain thing, your subconscious mind will eventually believe it's true, and it WILL truly become true.

# Topic 6

## THE FIRST FEW SECONDS ARE VERY IMPORTANT IN SALES

*Every second is of infinite value.*
   *- Johann von Goethe*

You have about four seconds before a prospect decides whether or not he or she likes what they see of you, and if they want to continue the process of listening to you. If they tolerate what they see and hear, they will give you another four to ten seconds to capture their interest. If you can keep the prospect's attention for about thirty seconds, and if they are willing to tolerate you for that short length of time, then that will set the stage as to whether or not they will buy from you. Here are several key methods that will increase your chances of the prospect warming up to you in those first few vital seconds.

### Build ease and rapport by complimenting the prospect the moment you meet them.

Most experts say you have between four to fifteen seconds to build that rapport before prospects lose interest in you and your message. Remember, they do not know you, so you must be quick in your effort to break the ice and build rapport. Don't let this fact scare you or make you nervous. Simply let the prospect see that you are just like them. Show them that you share the same interests they share, and that you like the same things they like. Compliment them on their watch, their car, their dog, their yard; their furniture– whatever presents itself as an opportunity for you to compliment them on, seek, find and use it to your advantage. Remember, a prospect will not buy from someone they don't like, or don't trust. Break the barrier by actively seeking and finding even some

12

common ground, or by complimenting them, so that you may build up that rapport.

## Mirror and match the prospect's exact natural behavior and movements – act the same way they act.

Strive to make this discovery as soon as possible – within five seconds – and continue for the next 1 to 4 or 6 minutes.

Keep in mind that anger, hostility and the likes do not include the natural behavior of a prospect, or anyone for that matter. *However, you may have to imitate subtly even those negative behaviors to make your point and be in synch with your prospect! Use your discretion.*

Flow with the prospect's customary demeanor – pick up on and mirror their natural movements, and position your body the same way they position theirs. Do this so that their subconscious mind may sense that you are both on the same page. Be careful not to come across as mocking or mimicking them – in fact, be subtle in all things, so they may not even detect that you are mirroring them.

If they are soft spoken, lower your voice. Laugh when they laugh, and smile when they smile. Pick up on the words that they use, and re-use those same words to your advantage. If they use the word "excellent," tell them about your "excellent" services. Whatever trait(s) the prospect may have, mirror it to make them feel that you are just like them; and that you both have much in common. This method is considered by many experts as one of the most powerful form of nonverbal persuasion.

## Always be yourself.

Your chances of being trusted or liked by a prospective buyer are greatly increased when you are simply being yourself. Yes, you must implement persuasive techniques and know your product well and be enthusiastic, but the foundation to a person liking you is due to being yourself with them. They will respect that of you. They will consider anything else as an insult to them. Being yourself with a prospect is simply non-verbally telling them that you're comfortable around them.

And who doesn't like the compliment of being told – in whatever manner – that they're comfortable to be around?

Think of being yourself as a cake and all of the other tactics as the icing on the cake. In other words, you must be yourself while enhancing that self with knowledge, patience, enthusiasm, conviction, persuasive techniques and all the other things that make a successful salesperson – or any person for that matter – successful.

## Always feel and be enthusiastic.

This is how you will win your prospect's interest – by your enthusiasm. Enthusiasm is contagious. Be as enthusiastic as a child would be – who has something to share with everyone; because they know that what they have to share is good. You should not expect your prospect to be enthused about your product if you yourself don't show enthusiasm. Don't force it. Let the product speak for itself by your enthusiasm for it.

Recall that feeling when you're enthusiastic about something, and be half that way. Don't be overly enthusiastic – because that in itself may be a turn off – but be as enthusiastic as is natural for you. If you're enthused, then the prospect will also be enthused. Everybody has been enthused about something at some time in their lives. Recall that enthusiasm of yours, and mirror it as you do your presentations in front of prospective buyers. Your job as a salesperson is to put on an act; to put on your best performance when the cameras start rolling. 5, 4, 3, 2, 1: ACTION! Approach each prospect with a fresh and inviting manner – as if they were your very first, and sole prospect!

## Always make your body language work for you.

Research shows that a prospect's decision upon whether they will like or trust you as a salesperson, and whether or not they will consider buying from you is determined by about 55% of your non-verbal communication, such as your facial expression and overall body language.

RELAX is the key word, and RELAX YOUR MIND, the key phrase towards overcoming any negative body language that you may carry. Get a massage, if need be, so you may know what it is and how it feels to be relaxed. Your muscles must not be tense in any part of your body – but your body language must be free and at ease at all levels. Carry yourself as an open book. Do not act in any unpredictable or sudden way. Feel comfortable in the way you carry yourself and be confident with your body.

Open up, and don't have any hidden agenda. Be as free as a bird. Walk, talk and act carefree. Show those around you that you are stress free – without worries or concerns. Show them that you don't have anything to hide because you don't; because you know that you and your product or service is good. Always be at ease. Be transparent. Behave as though you don't mind if your prospect sees through you because there's nothing to see; because you know that everything within you is clear as crystal, and yes, without blemish, of course.

Be the friendly neighbor who is comfortable to be around, as you yourself are just as comfortable to be around. Let the prospect feel at ease upon first seeing you, and upon the subsequent experience of being with you. *Relax your mind* is the key phrase. Let the prospect feel that relaxation vibe. Let them sense and know that they can trust you because you are a safe and friendly person to deal with. Make your image a non-judgmental one. Be non-threatening in all ways.

## Use a strong, powerful opening statement that captures the prospect's attention and that *clearly* states how they will benefit buying from you.

Give the prospect a logical and appetizing reason to want to buy your product or service. *"There are some discounts and new benefits that the company is offering.* If YOU have a few minutes, I can show YOU how YOU could save yourself some money." This is called a benefit statement. It is designed to capture the prospective buyer's attention and interest by making them curious about what you can do for them. This curiosity is usually activated by letting them know that you can do one or both of two things: 1) Save them money by reducing their current bill or by making it affordable for them, or 2) Provide them with a product or service that they need or want of great(er) value and reliability, even though it may cost more than what they were expecting.

## Plan to be persistent.

Persistency is the key to any hopes for you to become a successful salesperson. Research shows that about 60% of all prospects will say "No, I'm not interested" three times before they finally give in and say, "Ok, I'll try it."

Like an itch that must be constantly scratched, so must you be. Become a little aggressive – even somewhat annoying to deal with. You can't be too easy going if you plan to be a successful salesperson. Instead, you must be determined to the point where it is easier for the prospect to agree to your offer, than to be constantly "harassed" or "annoyed" by the persistent pest named you! Think of it – what have you got to lose by being a little persistent? Nothing! But on the other hand there is much to gain, such as that prospective customer becoming your real customer.

## Listen.

Show sincerity and concern for the prospect's interests. Let them feel and know that they are your main interest. Show them that you really care. What is the most effective way to show a prospect that you care? You accomplish this by listening to them. *At the front of your mind*, never look at your prospect as a number; instead look at each of them as separate individuals, with feelings and concerns.

## Ask pointed questions.

Always be on the prowl to ask specific questions that will lead you toward overcoming any prospective buyer's objections. Remember, you cannot overcome an objection if you don't know what that objection is. If they're not interested, simply ask them the two most logical questions in the world: "Why?" or, "Why not?" Investigate it until you find out the source or reason for the prospect's lack of interest. (The second most effective way to show a prospect that you really care is to ask them sincere questions.) See Topic 14.

## Show empathy.

Always put yourself into the prospect's shoes and walk a mile in them. Always try to understand their situation. Always see through their eyes. A prospect will be able to tell if you are being sincere; and that is what they will judge you by. Develop a sincere desire to want to help your prospect; and circumstances will see to it that you too will be taken care of automatically.

Always agree with the prospect who complains about you or your company's way of doing business. This will dramatically help you to build up credibility with them – and credibility and trust is what you want; for this is the key that makes good relationships. The prospect is always right. Whatever the prospect says, as a source of dissatisfaction, always say, "Yes, I agree with you. Others have also felt that way too, AND that is why we would like to make it up to you. We want to show you that we have changed; that we are not the same old company that we once were. We're a new company. We would like to know what we can do to make it better for you. Give me five minutes, and I will show you." Once the prospect sees or realizes that you're on their side and that you understand where they are coming from, then they will be more compelled to listen to you. They will feel obligated to give you a chance, for your consideration towards them.

❖

The first ten words out of your mouth are going to be more important than the next ten thousand. Timing and strategy are of prime importance when meeting the prospect for the first time. A speedy relationship must be built to ensure the end result is a new customer formed.

# Topic 7

---

# THE METHOD OF SELLING

*If you wish to win a man over to your ideas, first make him your friend.*
*- Abraham Lincoln*

To be successful in Sales you must have an organized method to get you through from points A to Z. From beginning to end, the method of selling will fall into these five stages below; and you will benefit greatly by paying close attention to them:

1.  **Build Rapport**
2.  **Promise**
3.  **Qualify**
4.  **Present**
5.  **Close**

## 1) <u>Build Rapport</u>:

The main purpose of building rapport is to SOFTEN the prospect's heart, so that they won't give you a hard time with rejections and objections. Building rapport includes:

✓  Putting the prospect at ease when first meeting and greeting them.

✓  Smiling and shaking the prospect's hand.

✓  Welcoming (or inviting) the prospect to your company.

✓  Identifying yourself to the prospect and asking them for their name.

✓  Finding something to break the ice, like a joke, a compliment, or identifying some type of common ground with the prospect to show them that you are just like them.

✓ Being in high spirits so the prospect may feed off of and reciprocate your cheerful mood.

If you've done a good job on building rapport then consider the sale at least 55% complete.

## 2) **Promise**:

Promise the prospect by using a *benefit statement* of either one or all of these four choices:

✓ Your offer is cheaper than the competition on a value basis and will save them money in the long run.
✓ Your offer is better than the competition and will save them headaches in the future.
✓ Your prospect will like your offer and will not regret it.
✓ If your prospect does not like your offer, you promise to not force something upon them they don't want or need. (But remember though that your job is to make the prospect DESIRE your offer, right?)

Living up to your promise creates a sense of trust within the prospect's mind towards you as a salesperson.

## 3) **Qualify**:

Qualify the prospect with interview-type questioning by:

✓ Directing the prospect to follow your lead.
✓ Letting the prospect know that you are going to ask them a couple of questions, and then ask them if that is ok. "If you don't mind, I'd like to ask you a couple of questions…"
✓ Finding out if the prospect is the decision maker.
✓ Finding out what the prospect's needs or wants are.

✓ Finding out if the prospect is able to financially afford the service you are offering. Match the prospect's financial situation to suit your product or service. If their budget is low, then plan to show them products or services that they will likely be able to afford.

✓ Discovering if there is anyone else in the prospect's family or within their circle of friends who may be INVOLVED or interested in the service you are providing.

✓ Asking the prospect what is most important to them about the service you are offering.

✓ Uncovering if the prospect is shopping around and with whom. (You need to know your competition.)

✓ Finding out and overcoming any objection that may be raised.

Asking the right questions shows the prospective buyer that you empathize with them and really care about their needs.

## 4) <u>Present</u>:

You will present your offer in an enthusiastic way as if you were offering a "delicacy" to someone who rightfully deserves it. Before showing the prospect your offer you will want to enhance their craving by using a benefit statement such as, "This is a good choice. I'll show you how you will lower your cost with this service." The steps are:

✓ Proudly introduce the history and mission statement of your company in a good light, especially if your company is not well known.

✓ Show the features of your product or service.

✓ Demonstrate the benefits of your offer. Features don't sell. Benefits do!

✓ Trial close by asking the prospect questions such as, "How does that sound?" "This is great, isn't it?"

✓ Involve the prospect in the presentation. Let them see, smell, feel, taste and hear your offer. Let them experience your service first hand. Let them bond with your service.

A good presentation ALWAYS answers the questions: "Why should the prospect buy from you?" and "What will they gain from it?"

## 5) <u>Close:</u>

The close should be considered the FINAL close since you were making many trial closes during your presentation, and ever since your first contact with the prospect.

✓  *Assume and act as if the prospect is ready to buy after your presentation, even if they haven't already agreed to your offer.* Use words and actions that indicate they said "yes", they'll take it!

✓  Enthusiastically give the prospect the cost for the service.

✓  Be silent immediately after saying or showing the prospect the price. Wait for them to speak first. (He who speaks first loses.)

✓  Make sure that you leave room for negotiation in your first and second price offers just in case the prospect wants to bargain.

✓  If the prospect is a *serial bargainer* then ask them the if/then question: If I can get you this for $X, then will you take this product home today?" If they say "yes" then ask them which method of payment they are using, "Cash, credit or check?" Ask for and take their method of payment and tell them you will see what you can do for them. Insist they show and give you their method of payment to show PROOF that they are serious and ready to buy if the price is right.

✓  If a prospect is not co-operating with you at all then ask them, "What do we need to do to earn your business today?" Ask them to give you a REASONABLE offer.

✓  Once the offer is accepted, summarize everything the prospect will be receiving and the price they will be paying.

A smooth close will be determined by how well you have followed the other steps that led up to the close.

❖

Keep in mind that the sales process always involves overcoming objections along the way and ABC, meaning to "Always Be Closing" with little trial closes.

Be sure to tailor and personalize ALL your sales experiences into an organized system that smoothly gets you through from points A to Z every time.

# Topic 8

---

## A CLOSER LOOK AT SOME SPECIFIC METHODS OF SELLING

*If you would persuade, you must appeal to interest rather than intellect.*
> *- Benjamin Franklin*

There are many things that you will need to take a closer look at when dealing with the method of selling. One of the most obvious is to know your product or service well. You must know the advantages and disadvantages your product or service has over and under the competition. Below are a few areas that dig beneath the surface of this wonderful iceberg known as selling:

### Avoid asking prospects close-ended questions to which they can respond "no" to, unless it's a "tag question" or you are otherwise probing for specific, personal data.

"Are you interested?" is a common mistake that salespeople often make. A question like, "What would you like to do?" is not a good choice either. Instead of asking these questions, ask them open-ended questions like, "How do you X?", or, "When would you X?", or, "When was X?" Examples: "When was the last time you had high-speed Internet?", or, "When would you be available for us to install your new water fountain, Tuesday or Thursday?" "How do you feel about getting a much better product that can save you time?" In this way, by giving them options you might be starting a conversation – or even better, getting them to make a decision – as opposed to getting a one worded "no" answer!

## Always know and point out that your offer or certain points about your offer is superior to the competition.

*Say good things about your competition, but say better things about your product/service.* Be sure to point out the superior features and emphasize the benefits of your product compared to the competition. Sometimes you may not be able to beat your competition in price but you will in quality and value.

Study, keep up-to-date with and know your facts well. Know both the weak and strong points of your competition – you must. Strive to have an answer for almost every question that comes at you.

Explain to the prospect the benefits of partaking in the opportunity of what you have to share with them. Don't just tell them about the features – show them benefits to these features. Appeal to their sense of sight, sound, taste, touch and smell. Let them see, smell, feel, taste or hear for themselves how what you have to offer will benefit them in their everyday life. But first, be sure to ask the specific question(s) that lets you know what exactly they are looking for, and what benefits they are looking for from that particular product or service. Why? You do not want to be showing features and benefits to a prospect who is not interested in those particulars; so, first find out what they are looking for most, then fire away on the benefits of those particular features.

## Always assume and remember to point out to your prospect that they can save lots of money on a value basis by accepting or switching to your service(s).

This is usually the main reason why a prospect will choose your product over their current situation – to achieve savings.

Ask them the *"If I/would you"* question: "If I could show you how to save up to $1,000 per year, would you be interested?" This form of questioning will often spark an interest within them!

*Always* ask them a generic question of this fashion to spark some type of interest within them. Give them examples of customers who have saved money by switching to your service.

24

## Start with *high-balled* price offers first and then if need be, gradually work your way down in price.

In sales it is unwise to start low because then there'd be no room to work your way back up. You can *always* go down in price but you can *never* go back up; this is a common negotiating rule.

Refrain from giving all your bargains in one shot. Hold back on the best or cheapest offer(s) for last – so that you may have something else to fall back on if all else fails. A prospect is more likely to purchase the cheaper – not cheapest – product if the most expensive one was introduced to them first. The point is, you at least got them to purchase something using this technique as opposed to purchasing nothing.

Remember, the average prospect will object at least three times before they give in to your offer, so you must be prepared to add at least four essential benefits or additional features or more discounts or a longer free trail period to your offer. Let them know that if they take your offer right now, the more they will be getting from it right now. Put a sweet taste in their mouth to make them want it right now.

## Create an urgency within your presentation to make the prospect act now.

Use words such as "limited offer" or "if you act today, you'll receive this discount" or "this offer is only good for today." People like scarcity. The harder it is to get something the more curious they become about it and the more they want it. That's human nature.

## A Method That Stands On Its Own: Be more determined to accomplish your purpose than the prospect is in accomplishing theirs.

Determination is the rage and anger that burns within you to achieve your success. Determination is the beginning and the end. Always focus on the purpose of why you're there with that prospect at that time and place – to make them buy! If you have not achieved that then you have not achieved your purpose. Remember, you're not there just for the sake or fun of it; you're there to accomplish something. And the only way that you can accomplish what you have set out for yourself is to be ragingly focused.

If you are not focused then you have forgotten your purpose, and you will not achieve the success you were looking for.

So be determined, with a *controlled* rage to finish what you have begun, with the aim of achieving or accomplishing the purpose for which you had set out for yourself. To achieve your goal, be very determined!

❖

Be sure to take a closer look at the method of selling to make the greater sense out of it all. And notice the flow of each aspect that leads to the other aspects.

# Topic 9

## THREE IMPORTANT THINGS TO ALWAYS REMEMBER IN SALES

*Wear a smile and have friends; wear a scowl and have wrinkles.*
  *- George Eliot*

*Politeness is an inexpensive way of making friends.*
  *- William Feather*

These are the three deeds that will melt many prospects hearts:

### 1) A SMILE

More important than the smile itself is the timing and the sincerity of the smile. You need not smile all the time but only at certain strategically important moments. It is good to smile upon first meeting a prospect and during certain highlights, such as when you're complimenting them or talking about some particularly fine features of your product or service. Additionally, if you are establishing some common ground with your prospect a smile to show you are in sync with them is beneficial.

With a sincere smile teeth are often slightly visible. Additionally, the expression reaches all the way up to the edges of the eyes.

A smile is important because it lets the recipient know there is something you like about them. And if you demonstrate a liking for the prospect, then they will reciprocate that feeling towards you by outwardly mirroring your smile back towards you or perhaps more subtly by feeling friendlier towards you.

If you have difficulties with this concept of smiling, then start out slowly. Instead of creating a big old smile on your face that HURTS, try a little smile. Make an effort to put a small, almost invisible smile on your face. For exercise purposes, try to hold this smile for about twenty seconds. After this exercise you will find that smiling may become something much easier to accomplish. In fact research has found that a simple smile can improve your overall mood to a more excitable and optimistic one.

## 2) A TOUCH, SUCH AS A HUG OR A HANDSHAKE

A touch provides a bond or an affinity between you and the person being touched. It creates a bond that speeds up the relationship into a friendlier one. It helps to break the barrier between both of you as strangers, creating a more responsive atmosphere. It brings both of you closer together. If you want someone to soften up more quickly then shake their hand or give them a hug, if appropriate.

Don't wait for the prospect to shake your hand – you should be the initiator by extending your hand first. Be sure to look into the prospect's eyes while shaking their hand. Make sure that your grip is firm but not tight. Say your name while you're shaking their hand, such as, "Hi! My name is Mark. And yours?"

**Note:** There is a condition wherein some people find their hands sweating uncontrollably when dealing with the public, or maybe even in private. This condition is known as Palmar Hyperhidrosis.

Indeed, it can be of great embarrassment and inconvenience.

Consider researching these four suggestions to mitigate this embarrassing and inconvenient problem:

1.  Beta Blockers for anxiety.
2.  Rubbing your hands with astringent oils.
3.  An expensive operation called the Endoscopic Thoracic Sympathectomy, which can have side effects.
4.  Iontophoresis therapy, which can be administered from a hospital or purchased for home use.

## 3) ASKING FOR, REMEMBERING AND CALLING PROSPECTS BY THEIR FIRST NAMES

The sweetest sound to a person's ears that grabs their attention more than any other word is their name. Gently calling a person by their name puts them to attention and makes them feel good, and gives them a sense of being important. When you warmly call someone by their name they are more likely to pay attention to what you have to say. It also creates within them the warm feeling that is associated with being appreciated. A person's name warmly being called by another person will make them feel appreciated, important and special. It will definitely attract their attention.

An experienced salesperson will put forth extra effort to get a prospect's name, remembering and using it to let the prospect know that they are important.

A good way to remember a person's name is to write it down as soon as possible. Repeating the name multiple times after first hearing it will also help you remember it. Associating that person's name with something or someone else that you know will also enhance your ability to remember their name.

Ask your prospect's permission to use their first name. For example, if the prospect's name is Juanita Merchant, ask her permission to use her first name, or if she would like to be called by her first name. Additionally, if the prospect's name is Michael or Elizabeth, for example, ask if it's okay to call them "Mike" or "Liz" or would they prefer their full name instead.

Be sure not to overuse the prospect's name. Use it as it would be natural to use. For example, using it three times within a half hour timeframe would be sufficient. Once upon introduction by repeating their name back to them as they tell you what it is and twice more during your normal half hour conversation. As time goes by, their name should be used less frequently.

❖

These are the three simple yet powerful deeds that will be the beginning to a fruitful start in catering to a prospect's buy mode.

# Topic 10

---

## HOW TO BUILD RAPPORT FOR SURE

*If a man is worth knowing at all, he is worth knowing well.*
*- Alexander Smith*

A good conversation builds rapport. You can quickly build verbal rapport by merely asking your prospect these five rapport-building questions:

1.  **What do you do for a living?**
2.  **Do you have a family?**
3.  **What do you *like to* do for fun?**
4.  **How's your neighborhood?**
5.  **Do you know of a good place to go for vacation?**

**1) *Why asking, "What do you do for a living?" builds rapport:***
People like to brag about themselves even if they have nothing to brag about. The fact that you are curious enough about them to ask this question will generally make them feel special.

**2) *Why asking, "Do you have a family?" builds rapport:***
People especially like to brag about their children as well as other family members, including their spouse. They consider these people as the trophies of their lives. Bringing up this topic will make them feel special. And making someone feel special builds rapport.

**3) *Why asking, "What do you like to do for fun?" builds rapport:***
People like to think about what's fun for them. Asking this question will make them think of the same feelings of excitement, almost as if they were right there, doing what they love. Friends ask such questions. Asking this question puts you on a friendlier level with a prospect. They

30

may even invite you to join them.

### 4) *Why asking, "How's your neighborhood?" builds rapport:*
Even if a person does not like where they live or their living arrangements, it is still the only place they know as home. Their neighborhood is their home. Asking such a question is inviting yourself into that person's home. This question extends the relationship between both of you to a more personal one. You will become a part of their homely environment. They may even think about inviting you to their neighborhood – perhaps for a meal at a fine restaurant.

### 5) *Why asking, "Do you know of a good place to go for vacation?" builds rapport:*
Almost everybody loves taking or talking about taking vacations at some point or another. They also like the fact of being in the position to *recommend* things to others. This question of yours will conjure up pleasant memories within the prospect's mind. They will associate those pleasant feelings with the person who asked them to release these special feelings and images within their mind. They will love the idea of giving you some good ideas too. But if you think this vacation question is too broad, you may want to ask a more local question like, "Do you know of a good restaurant to go for dinner?"

❖

On the other side of this spectrum, you do not want to ask questions that sound too personal like, "Are you married?"or "Do you have any children?"or "Who do you live with?" Remember, it's not what you say but how you phrase it that's going to make the real difference. These same questions can be asked in a way so that the prospect will not ask, "What business is that of yours?"

But don't just ask these five basic questions – follow up by asking additional questions and by adding your own input into the conversation. Become indulged and fascinated with the conversation. Use such words as, "wow" or "that's interesting." Ask them their children's ages and so forth. Add to the conversation rather than taking it silently to heart. Follow these guidelines and building rapport will become second nature to you, for sure.

# Topic 11

---

## THE SIX MAIN REASONS WHY A PROSPECT WILL *NOT* WANT TO BUY

*All our reasoning ends in surrender to feeling*
*- Blaise Pascal*

In order to understand what will make a prospect buy, you must also understand what will make them not buy. Here are the six main objections that a prospect will present to not buy:

1. *Price. They think the price is too high.*
2. *They want to shop around.*
3. *They need to speak to someone else: husband/wife.*
4. *They don't like your product or service.*
5. *They don't like you.*
6. *They're happy with what they have.*

---

**1) Price. They think the price is too high.**
Ask the prospect, "Other than price, is there anything else that is keeping you from taking this product home today?" If they say "no," then you'll know to focus your close on price negotiation. Refer to Topic 67 – *A Closer Look at Negotiating Price.*

**2) They want to shop around.**
   a. If you are the *first* place/person they've been to, let them know that their *first choice*, like instinct, is always the best. Let them know, "Destiny brought you here." Tell them they might develop a lot of pleasant experiences with your product or service.

33

b.  If you are the *second* place/person they've been to, let them know, "Well at least now you have something to compare with" and as they can clearly see, your product outperforms the competition by a huge margin.

c.  If you are the *third* place/person they've been to, let them know, "third time's a charm." Explain to them that the third choice is a sign of luck. They may get lucky in other ways if they choose your product or service today.

d.  If you are the *fourth* place/person they've been to, let them know, "It's not wise to shop around at too many places because you will miss out on some important things that you really like." Inform them how looking too much will actually make them end up choosing something that they may not like. Show them that they must follow their instinct and choose the product or service that feels right. "Too much shopping around will make you forget the main things that make you happy."

e.  If you are the *fifth* place/person they've been to, let them know, "A good diamond has five sides," and your product will be the precious stone of their shopping experience. Remind them of the lucky number 5.

## 3) They need to speak to someone else: husband/wife.

If the prospect says they need to speak to someone else such as their husband or wife for advice then let them know that it is better for them to take your product home with them to show it to their advisor. Explain the company's courtesy policy of allowing them to take the product home without officially buying it yet. If they don't like it they can always return it risk free, right?

## 4) They don't like your product or service.

To discover if the prospect likes the product or service you are offering ask them, "From a scale of 1 to 10 – 10 being the best – how do you like the product?" If their answer is less than 7 you may want to show them something else before negotiating price. They must love the product if the sale is to be a smooth one. You may also want to review how you are presenting the features and benefits of your product or service.

## 5) They don't like you.

If you don't feel a connection with the prospect, then you were probably not successful in building rapport. If a prospect does not like you they will not buy anything from you unless they have to. Refer to Topic 10 – *How To Build Rapport.*

## 6) They're happy with what they have.

If the prospect says they're happy with their current product or service ask them, "If there was one thing you would change about your current product, what would it be?" Depending on their answer, tailor your presentation accordingly.

Ask your prospect, "What do you like most about your current service?" to discover your competitor's strengths. Whatever their answer is try to show them twice as many benefits in your product or service. Demonstrate why your product is so much better and how it will make them feel so much better by claiming it.

The bottom line to overcoming a prospect's lack of will to buy something is to make them *feel good* about the thought of buying. In almost every situation *feelings* out weigh reasoning. Make the prospect's experience a fun one.

Do have fun as you learn to overcome the six main objections why prospects will not want to buy.

# Topic 12

---

## DISCOVER HOW TO OVERCOME THOSE ANNOYING OBJECTIONS

*If you would convince others, seem open to conviction yourself.*
        *- Lord Chesterfield*

Objections and rejections are the two main enemies in the life of any salesperson. Here are some methods – thanks to the help of ChangingMinds.org – that will relieve the gripping hands of defiance:

### Boomerang:

Use what the prospect says back at them. To the prospect who says that your product is too expensive or they could find something cheaper, say: "Yes, I know it's expensive and I think you would prefer something of better quality for yourself. You deserve it, don't you think? Sometimes in the long-run the cheapest things turn out to be more expensive than the expensive ones!" When the prospect says something, (or if they said something that was beneficial to you), use it to your advantage: "You said X." Example: "You said your main priority was to save money. Well here it is – you'll be saving this amount of money every year!"

### Deflection:

With this method you will be avoiding their objection so that you can proceed with your presentation. For example: "I see." "I understand." "I know." "I'll get to that in a few minutes." By acknowledging that you hear and understand the prospect's concern and by giving the suggestion that you will get back to it at a more convenient time, the prospect may "give you a break" in this particular situation. If you are a persistent salesperson then you will need to do a lot of deflecting if you intend to get your message across.

## Feel, Felt, Found:

This is the classical method of dealing with a disgruntled prospect's objection(s). When you are faced with a prospect who is dissatisfied with your service, probably because they've had a bad experience with your company in the past, then this is where the *feel, felt found* method comes in.

The *feel, felt, found* method acknowledges to the prospect that you understand how they *feel*; that other people have *felt* the same way they're feeling – so that they know they're not alone; and that after experiencing your company's service again, those same people *found* something unexpected – something desirable about the services offered. For example: "Yes, I understand how you *feel*. Others have *felt* that way before, but after trying out our new services, they've *found* it to be one of the most reliable services they've ever experienced."

## Justification:

With this method your aim is not to disagree with a prospect, but rather to agree with their objection plus give them an explanation. Give a reasonable and logical explanation as to why so is so. "Yes, that's why we X – because X." Example, "Yes, that's why we charge you extra – because it's a much better quality." or "Yes, it has a small flaw, but that's why you're getting such a give-away discount."

## LAIR: Listen, Acknowledge, Identify objection, Reverse it.

Handle the prospect's objection by demonstrating that you're totally aware of their situation. "Yes, I know that you X because X, right? That's why X."

After you have acknowledged and identified their specific objection by specifically reiterating it back to them, then reverse it. When they tell you their objection, then reply, "Yes I know that you have a satellite dish and you don't want to change anything. You don't want to change anything because you are satisfied with your dish service, right? Good. Well that's why I'm here – to let you know about some things / features / benefits / savings that you may not be aware of about us." Or, "Yes, I know you need to shop around because you want to see what your options are, right? That's okay. That's why we're going to give you the least expensive price possible with the best service. This way, you may not need to shop around."

## Pre-empting:

Deliberately point out minor or major faults in your product or service before the prospect does. They must be made aware that nothing is 100% perfect. This will increase your credibility as a salesperson because everybody knows that nothing is perfect – and so do you. Tell your prospect(s) about some of the minor faults or setbacks of the service that you are offering to them. This will actually help to build up trust and credibility towards you as a salesperson. The prospect will look at you more as a friend because friends sometimes tell us the things that we may not want to hear – but thankfully, they tell us the truth for our own good that we should hear. If the fault in your product is obvious, then be quick to point it out to the prospect before they mention it to you. By doing this you will lessen the potency of that faultiness. However be sure to give a good reason, or an extra benefit of your product or service that overrides the faultiness. "This water-cooler uses a lot of electricity but the good news is that you won't have the inconvenience of having to stock huge amounts of bottled water in your cupboards."

## Reframing:

Reframing an objection is in essence turning the prospect's "no" into your misunderstanding so that you won't be interrupted while selling to them. Reframing an objection is basically turning that negative into something positive on purpose. Do not acknowledge their objection – instead treat it as if you did not hear them correctly or as if you misunderstood them. For example, use a phrase such as, "That's great, isn't it?" when they complain about it being "too big." or "Let me put it this way..." to suggest that they will agree with you if you explain it to them another way. "I can see this is not making sense to you. Let me put it this way..." If they complain that it's "awful," let them know that it will be perfect for them because they will make it great. "Yes, it's awfully beautiful, right? You'll make it beautiful."

# Renaming:

Objections use specific words and phrases, such as "not interested," "costs too much," "too complicated," etc. By changing the words or phrases used in the objection to your advantage you can actually change the meaning of the objection; thus changing the prospect's perception or view point of their *own* objection. For example if a prospect says, "It's too big," you may say, "too big" is another way of saying "spacious." And spacious means your prospect will have "more room" when they need it, so they won't have to worry about space later on. Another example, the prospect says they're worried about making a decision too quickly – you can change the word "worried" to "excited." Thus your response could be: "Worried can be summed up as being excited. Feeling excited is natural; it's a good thing. That's what motivates people. Go ahead and take it home today... You'll feel really good and excited about your decision."

I encourage you to write a list of all the common objections and excuses that a prospect will give to you, and think about comeback words that will transform the meaning of there objections. Following are some examples:

| Change Objections From | | To |
|---|---|---|
| Too expensive | _____ | Holds value |
| Too small | _____ | Neat and compact |
| Dissatisfied | _____ | Legitimate concerns |
| Shop around | _____ | Curious |
| Not interested | _____ | Busy |
| Undecided | _____ | Anxious and excited |

## Reprioritizing:

Lower the standards for why they like something. Show them that there is a better way to look at it. Diminish their priorities as being less important than the re-priority that you are about to share with them. At the same time build up your re-priority as something greater than their priority. "I know you want to look around but have you considered the stress associated with looking around and then choosing something that you may later regret? Now that you are in this fresh mode, let's choose what seems best for you! The first choice is usually the best." Another one is, "I understand price is an important factor in your decision, but shouldn't you be focused more on value over price with such an important product like this? I understand price is an important factor in your decision but how wise do you think it would be with such an important product like this? And how much wiser do you think it would be, with such an important product like this, that you should be focused more on value over price? With a product like this, quality is definitely more important that price, isn't it?

❖

Turn a prospect's objections into a game of life that you are more than willing to play!

# Topic 13

---

## TWENTY-FIVE WAYS TO CLOSE A SALE

*The door of opportunity won't open unless you do some pushing.*
  *- Anonymous*

A countless plethora of closing techniques exist, indeed, for us to experiment with. Thanks to the help of the website, *ChangingMinds.org*, the names of a host of closing techniques are listed below. In general, you must not look at a *close* as something that should only be attempted at the end of your presentation. Indeed, you should always be trying to find a way to close the sale and attempting to close that sale from the moment of contact right through to the end of your presentation.

**1) The 1-2-3 Close:** Highlight three things in a row about your product or service that are valuable, beneficial or better than the competition. This is in essence giving the prospect three good reasons to buy your product. It also summarizes your product with three key words or phrases. For example: "Well as you can see, our services may not be cheaper but we have better quality, faster speed, and more reliability."

**2) The Adjournment Close:** If you reckon the prospect is definitely not ready then make an appointment for a more convenient time. For instance, if the decision maker is not available you will need to make an appointment to see him or her later on. Ask your current prospect, "What's a good day for both of you?" "What time? Would Thursday at 4:15pm be good or is 7:45 pm better for you?" "When will the decision maker be available?" "What's their name and number?" "I know you need to think about it so I'll give you some time. We can talk on Tuesday at 10:15 am – how's that?"

**3) <u>The Assumptive Close</u>:** This is a favorite close of many experienced salespeople. With this close you do not wait for the prospect to make a decision. Instead you make the decision for them by the assumption that they want your services. And so your actions therefore are as if they had said "yes" they want it.

Don't wait for the prospect to agree to the sale— consider the sale as already having been made until they choose to interrupt your assumption. Follow up your presentation with a contract agreement even though the prospect has not yet verbally agreed to your offer. Ask the prospect at what time they would like to have their product delivered at their home, if not right now. Ask them if they need assistance taking their product home or if they can manage on their own. "Is 2 o'clock today good or is 5pm tomorrow better?"

Another assumptive close is to say the price then ask them this question: "Will you be using cash, credit or check for this purchase?" Do not give them the option of saying "yes" or "no" to your proposal but give them an option of how they are going to claim your offer.

**4) <u>The Bracket Close</u>:** Give your prospect three offers, with your target item in the middle. Show them the most expensive item first without letting them know about the other two. When they say it's too expensive then show them the second item which is closer to their budget. If they still seem unsure then show them the third item which is the cheapest and has the least value of all.

When given the choice of three options a prospect is most likely to choose the item in the middle because it almost always seems to be the most logical choice to make.

**5) <u>The Companion Close</u>:** Find out if anyone else with the prospect is interested in your offer. If the answer is yes then you can use that to your advantage by selling to the person who is with your prospect. "Your daughter seems to like it." "Why don't you do it for her?" Encourage the other person to persuade your prime prospect to consider the offer.

If your prospect does not have a companion present then allow yourself to speak for the companion. "Your daughter will love this."

Some prospects may be sensitive to the fact that you are using their companion to persuade them to do something they may not want to do, so don't be too obvious with this approach. Be subtle.

**6) The Compliment Close:** Constantly scan around your prospect's world to determine the things about them that stand out and which you think are likable. Make sincere compliments about anything concerning them that is worth complimenting. In general, people like to be complimented on their sense of style and intelligence, but don't overdo it. For example: "I like that watch very much. Where did you get it? Is that a Rolex? Wow! Nice!"

**7) The Conditional Close:** If there is some obstacle in the way that's preventing the prospect from making a decision then ask them the *"If I X, would you X?"* question: "If I can get you this refrigerator for $950 instead of $1,100, would you take it home today?"

This close asks the question of if you do something special for the prospect, would they do something for you in return. It gets to the bottom of what would make the prospect act according to your desire. It encourages the prospect to say "yes" on a middle ground offer.

**8) The Demonstration Close:** Utilize your knowledge and body to show the prospect how your product works. Seeing is believing, as a picture is worth a thousand words. A demonstration of your product is proof that it works as you claim it does. Let the product speak for itself by demonstrating it to the best of your abilities. "Let me show you how this works…"

**9) The Distraction Close:** An example of the distraction close would be to write the order while you're presenting to the prospect. Tell them that you want them to see on paper just how much they would be paying so they can get a clearer picture. After showing them the paper with all the calculations, ask them if this looks reasonable to them. If it does, request that they put their autograph on it. This is one form of the distraction close. The bottom line with the distraction close is to find a way to not allow the prospect to distract you from making a sale – instead you are distracting the prospect by slowly doing things that eases the sale along. In this case you are writing up the order while they're saying they're not buying now. You will reply by saying, "I know. I want you to see what you will be paying." Now after all your work on paper and after showing them the facts, all they have to do is sign on the dotted line.

**10) <u>The Economic Close</u>:** Enthusiastically inform your prospect that you can save them money. If savings is not obvious in the short run then show the prospect how they will be saving money in the long run. For example, if your product or service is relatively expensive show them how much money they will be saving per year rather than per month. Show them how they will be saving money over time. "I know this item may seem expensive but with the extra warranty it carries and the durable material it is made, you won't have to replace it year after year, and you will actually be saving money over time."

**11) <u>The Emotion Close</u>:** Most people buy on an emotional basis. They buy mostly because of want, not need. Therefore you must use that fact to your advantage by finding out what it is about your product that triggers your prospect's emotional wants. For example: "I know you're dissatisfied when your X doesn't work, that's why you'll enjoy the comfort of our X." or "I know you like X, so here's a lot of X for you to enjoy." Then try to get the prospect to act right away, before they change their mind.

**12) <u>The IQ Close</u>:** Suggest to your prospect that most people who buy your product or service are somehow more intelligent than other people. Make them feel as if they are making an intelligent decision by agreeing to your proposal. "I can see you're an intelligent customer, Mr. Smith, and that's the reason why I know this product will be good for you." "Most people who buy this product are well informed." "A college principal bought this very same product last week."

**13) <u>The Ownership Close</u>:** This close shares a similarity with the assumptive close. Let the prospect feel and think they have already purchased your product by labeling it as *theirs*. "How do you like your new car, Mr. Smith?" "This is yours." "It's you." "It fits you just right!" "It looks good on you." "Just picture your new car in your driveway."

**14) <u>The Puppy Close</u>:** With this close you are trying to make the prospect feel an emotional connection with your product by letting them have it for free, temporarily. You are trying to create an *attachment* between the customer and the product so the prospect will not want to bring it back after they have become used to and attached to it. "Take this home for a few days and see if you like it. If you don't, just bring it back. You'll get a complete refund."

The puppy close got its name from pet sellers who would try to get their customers to take a puppy home just to see if they liked them, with the promise to take them back if the customer did not like the puppy. The pet sellers knew the customers would more than likely develop an attachment with the puppy and not want to bring them back. The sale would then be made.

**15) <u>The Quality Close</u>:** Sometimes you won't be able to beat the competition on price and this is where quality comes in. Let your prospect know that value is priceless and that they must not devalue their experience by getting something cheap and less reliable. "The cheaper products break down easily. However with this item you will have a longer lasting product that will give you trouble free service year after year. It's worth the extra money."

**16) <u>The Referral Discount Close</u>:** Inform your prospect that you will give them an extra discount if they provide you with the name(s) and number(s) of one or two referrals. Though you may have been able to give them a discount regardless, tag this as the referral discount to inspire them and to provoke you into getting more customers. "If you can write down the name and number of one or two referrals then I will be able to give you our referral program discount."

**17) <u>The Repetition Close</u>:** Repeating yourself over and over again will psychologically annoy the prospect into submission. Use different words and phrases during your presentation to make them submit under pressure. For example: "Take it now," "Take it home," "It's yours," "Sign here," "Don't wait," "Let's do it now" and "Now is the best time to buy." Wear the prospect out by constantly nagging and telling them to claim the offer now. Make them give in to your request by saying the same thing over and over again. Repetition will make many prospects submit to your commands or requests. The average prospect will give in at about the fourth close.

**18) <u>The Reversal Close</u>:** At times you may have to back off to move forward. Sometimes you may just have to take it slow or even go in a totally opposite direction if you want to make progress and speed things up. Tell a vacillating prospect, "You may not like this product." "This may not be for you." When the prospect realizes they are not being pressured they might feel an obligation to go ahead with a purchase. Your prospect might develop an urge to walk towards a sale as opposed to walking away or sense that they might be missing out on something special if they don't act now.

People like what they can't have or that which they are told they can't have. Their defiance will make them want to do the opposite of what you say.

**19) <u>The Selective-Deafness Close</u>:** If a prospect brings up a topic that you cannot handle or an issue that you cannot resolve via your product or service then focus on the other issues that may be beneficial to them. You may want to ignore the issue they bring up altogether by skillfully changing the topic, acting as if you misunderstood the question or by answering in a way that is to your benefit. If the prospect is objecting to your offer you may want to change the topic by complimenting something about them. "I'm not interested," says the prospect. "That's a very nice watch you're wearing there. Where did you get it?" or "Did you say you work for a diamond collector?" Switching the conversation from their objection to your choice of discussion will put you back in control of the situation.

**20) <u>The Standing-Room-Only Close</u>:** Let the prospect know your product is selling like hot cakes and that everyone wants to get a piece of the action. Price is not an issue with a product like this. Make them want to jump on the bandwagon. "A lot of people are signing up now because they see the benefits."

**21) <u>The Testimonial Close</u>:** Prospects want to know about other people's experiences with your product or service. Ease their concerns and lessen their worries by giving them responses from people who have and love what you are offering.

Tell the prospect a compelling story of a customer who was skeptical at first but after trying out your product, wished they had done so long before. "I had a customer who recently purchased our product and they just love it. They told me how at first they were so skeptical but now they wished they had purchased it years ago." If at all possible provide your prospect with evidence.

**22) <u>The Treat Close</u>:** If a prospect is unable to find any reasons to purchase your product or service then use the treat close on them. Make them feel as if they are giving themselves a gift by accepting your offer. Let them feel as if they are treating themselves to something desirable. "You deserve it. Consider it your birthday present. Have fun with it."

**23) <u>The Trial Close</u>:** The trial close is not a direct close in itself, but a test to see how far you are from closing the sale.

During the presentation it is important to periodically get a feel as to how much the prospect is agreeing to your offer. "How does that sound?" "That's good, right?" "Isn't that great?" The trial close is also referred to as the ABC of closes: *Always Be Closing*. However beware of another ABC: *Also Be Careful* not to annoy your prospect out of the sale with too many trial closes.

**24) <u>The Ultimatum Close</u>:** Put a little fear in the prospect's mind. Make them think there will be regretful, missed opportunities by not accepting or delaying their purchase.

"If you don't X, then X" For example, "If you don't buy this now then the price is going to rise soon," "If you don't take it home today then someone else might take it away" or "If you don't take advantage of this opportunity then you'll still be having the same problems with your current service."

**25) <u>The Valuable Customer Close</u>:** Make an offer to the prospect that is only for a "selected few." Since they are the "valuable customer," offer your extra bonus, gift or discount because they are your valued customer. Make them feel special and treat them appropriately because they are special.

❖

Someone said once that the definition of a *close* is simply *a bad presentation.* In other words, you should not be thinking about closing at the end of a presentation – you should be writing up the order after your spectacular presentation, which was the close in itself. Be sure to close your deals before your prospects close their hearts on the sale!

# Topic 14

## TEN VERY POWERFUL QUESTIONS TO ASK PROSPECTS!

*Millions saw the apple fall, but Newton was the one who asked why.*
  *- Bernard Mannes Baruch*

Knowing what questions to ask your prospect is a major step towards influencing their decision to buy. In other words, the types of questions you ask can make or break a sale. Certain questions will set the stage to make the prospect answer "yes." These questions will make something click in their head. When persuading others to buy, very often a question *asked* is more important than an answer given. The question itself will make them decide to buy!

1.  **Why?** or **Why not?**

2.  **What is the one thing you would like to improve about X** ("your current service(s), or, condition," for example)**?**

3.  **If I X** ("could get you this price you're looking for," for example)**, would you X** ("be interested, or, sign up today," for example)**?**

4.  **What is preventing you from X** ("acting right now," for example)**, or, What is holding you back from X** ("acting now," for example)**, or, Besides price, is there anything else that would prevent you from taking this today – if it were free would you take it?**

5.  **What do WE need to do X** ("to earn your business today, or, for you to come to a decision today," for example)**?**

6.  **What is it that you like most about X** ("your current service," for example**), or, What is most important to you about X?**

7.  **From a scale of one to ten, ten being the best, X** ("how do you like this product," for example**)?**

8.  **How do you know that X** ("your needs are being satisfied, or, you're getting the best service for your money, or, you won't be interested in what I have to say," for example**)?**

9.  **Which do you prefer, X or Y** ("signing with this pen or that one," for example**)?**

10. **If it were completely up to you, would you X** ("take this offer right now, or, agree to the sale today," for example)**?**

## Why These Questions Are Powerful:

1.  **"Why?" or "Why not?":**
    When you first meet someone you usually greet them by saying something like, "Hi." In the same manner when someone rejects your offer, your first instinct is to ask the most logical question in the world: "Why?" Always make your first question, "Why?" or "Why not?" when a prospect rejects your offer.

    This is important: When you ask the questions why or why not, ask them as if surprised or confused; as if the person is not being rational by rejecting your offer. The way you respond will be important towards making an effective impression in the prospect's subconscious mind. One cannot know the cause of a problem unless one asks the question, "Why?"

2.  **"What is the one thing you would like to improve about X** (your current service(s), or, condition, for example)**?":**
    This is one of the best questions because it forces them to think of something that they don't like about their current service or product – something they would like to change about their situation. Since

most people don't like change, you must provide them with a good reason to change. However, with this question, you are not the one actually providing them with a reason to change – you are allowing them to think on their own for a reason to change. Once this has been accomplished your job as a salesperson becomes a lot easier in persuading your prospect.

3. **"If I X** (could get you this price that you're looking for, for example)**, would you X** (be interested, or, sign up today, for example)**?":**
This question is a challenge of sorts to the prospect. You are allowing them to make a decision if you can do something for them. It's only fair. If you can come up with your part of the bargain, so should they.

4. **"What is preventing you from X** (acting right now, for example)**"**, or, **"What is holding you back from X** (acting now, for example)**?"** or **"What is the one main reason why you would not X** (be interested, or, want to buy, for example) or, **"Besides price, is there anything else that would prevent you from taking this today – if it were free would you take it?":**
You cannot solve a problem unless you know what the problem is. The prospect most likely knows what the problem is, or at least they should. Ask them what is preventing them from making a decision. Let them search deep within their soul, if need be, to find out what is holding them back from making a decision. Once the reason is given, be prepared to resolve their objection. If your offer was for free, would they take it even then, is a question that you must get the answer to.

5. **"What do we need to do X** (to earn your business today, or, for you to come to a decision today, for example)**?":**
This question puts the situation into the prospect's hands. It asks them what would make them agree or say "yes" to the sale. It implies that there is something that will cinch the deal and asks what it is. (Every customer has a price.) Notice how the question asks, "What

do we…" and not, "What do I…" Remember, it's never about you as the salesperson, but rather about them as a satisfied customer.

6. **"What is it that you like most about X** (your current service, for example)**?", or, "What is most important to you about X** (your current service(s), for example)**", or, "Why did you choose X** (your current situation, for example)**?":**
This question investigates why the prospect likes what they have, or don't have yet. Once you understand what makes them like what they have, or are considering having, you can use that information to your advantage to persuade them that you have exactly what they're looking for.

7. **"From a scale of one to ten, ten being the best, X** (how do you like this product, for example)**?":**
This is a question that should be used all the time. In hospitals, when a patient is in pain or depressed the nurse or doctor usually asks them, "From a scale of 1 to 10, how bad is the pain or how do you feel – with 10 being the worst?" In the same manner, use this scale in the reverse format to find out where you are with your prospects. The number they give you will tell you how near or far away you are from making a sale.

   If the prospect answers that their liking for your product or service is less than ten, then ask them, "What would make it a ten?" Then tailor your presentation to fulfill that ten. Furthermore, if the prospective buyer says their interest is less than a seven, then you may need to switch your product or service to something else if you can.

8. **"How do you know that X** (your needs are being satisfied, or, you're getting the best service for your money, or, you won't be interested in what I have to say, for example)**?":**
This question challenges the prospect's belief system. In other words, what they may have thought was true, may not in fact be true.  An

effective way to change a person's perception is to show them that what they once thought was true or factual, may not actually be the case. Though people don't like to be perceived as being wrong, it is better to point this out than for them to reject your offer based on faulty information.

9. **"Which do you prefer, X or Y** (signing with this pen or that one, for example)**?":**
This question gives the prospect an option – a choice. And choices are what most prospects like. To be effective, the options being offered should in fact be very similar and the selection of either choice should bring you the same basic end result. Most people will look at two options as being something totally different from the other. Use this knowledge to your advantage by presenting two or more options that will ensure you the same end result.

10. **"If it was completely up to you, would you X** (take this offer right now, or, agree to the sale today, for example)**?":**
If the prospect is hesitant or can't make up their mind or if they say they must consult someone before making a decision, ask them this question. You may try saying, "Do you like this product?" If they say "yes", then try responding with, "Well since you like it and the only objection you have is to speak with your husband first, what we'll do is let you have it now. This way you can show it to your husband while getting the savings today. If your husband doesn't like it then we'll take it back at no cost to you. Sounds fair? Please autograph your name here.

❖

Questions can make a world of difference in the mind of a prospect.

# Topic 15

---

## TRAIN YOURSELF TO THINK POSITIVELY

*Change your thoughts and you change your world.*
    *- Norman Vincent Peale*

*Pain is inevitable. Suffering is optional.*
    *- Anonymous*

This topic is a preview of other things to come. Many of these subjects are discussed in further depth on other pages; but these have been written to give you a snapshot of the mindset of a positive salesperson. Your attitude is the key that will turn the lock to open the door of success, or keep it shut forever.

### Always think positively.

Your success as a salesperson will be solely dependant and determined by how positive you are. Every success you will ever have will revolve around your world of positive thinking. Every successful move or achievement will be reflected in how positive you were in that particular moment in time. Any negativity from you will breathe failure like a swarm of larva turned into mosquitoes. Each negative thought will tear you down with it and will devour everything you worked so hard to build up. Think positively always. You owe it to yourself to always think positively!

### Always be confident.

Doubt drives away your potential customers. You will attract whatever you fear if you keep on worrying about it.

Don't panic if you're not making any sales. Every salesperson goes through the ebbs and flow of Sales that go up and down like the waves of the ocean. Don't lose your confidence when the waves of your Sales go down. Confidence is the belief that you will ultimately succeed in your efforts no matter how bad your current conditions are. Confidence is staying strong in spite of obstacles placed in your way. For a salesperson, confidence is the belief that you're going to make a sale or another sale soon, even if you haven't made one recently. You must ride on the waves of Sales rather than drown in them.

## Feel lucky, not unlucky.
Rid yourself of self-pity, doubt and despair, and spare yourself the grief; and this will be all the luck you will need. But feel confident with yourself and your circumstances, and the universe will take good care of you. Think positively and a positive reaction will charge you. The best time to feel lucky is during those times when you find yourself constantly running into no luck at all – and then you would have defeated the mystery of luck itself.

## Enjoy what you do.
Turn every stress and worry into something too little to take away your overall joy. Let each situation take care of itself. Use your heart mostly, rather than your head and it will show. Consider your job as a good marriage, to hold, cherish and love in good times and bad. If you can't find a way to love what you do then consider a divorce.

## Consider yourself an authority.
Like a doctor, see it as your job to let the prospect know that you are the one who knows what's best for them. See yourself as a person of authority because a profession in Sales is the position of authority. You have every right to be there at that time and place, with that person. Never look at yourself as an intruder, but rather a problem solver who has come because you know what is best for the prospect.

## Believe in what you do as if it were your religion, with a strong intent to achieve success.

Take your job very seriously and don't just do it because it's your job or because you were told to do it. Instead do it because you know you'll personally make the difference in each prospect's life. Believe strongly in your product and defend it, even though it may have its faults because nothing is perfect. And stand up for it like you would your beloved friend, and inevitably your prospect will pick up on your conviction. Put your doubt in a suitcase and walk with a strong belief and a burning desire for what you do.

## Feel like a winner.

How does a winner feel? It is more than just the opposite of how a loser feels. Winners like to play the games they're good at and brag about winning the next bet. Therefore, always be up to the challenge of winning the next big bet.

Furthermore, in your efforts to win the next big bet, take a little time now and list three things you have achieved in the last five to ten years – things that made you feel like a winner. Here are some scenarios to assist you:

a. Finally getting the money or loan and a chance to purchase something that you were wishing to have for the longest time, like a certain car, home, television or watch.

b. Graduating from something or somewhere that was not easy to get through, like a course, a class or a college.

c. Finally losing *or gaining* weight that you were aiming for, whether it was ten pounds or two hundred pounds.

d. Finally getting up and deciding to do something that you have been procrastinating about for the longest while, like drinking more water, visiting your doctor more frequently, going to the gym, going out and having more fun or just restraining yourself and having less fun by taking care of your priorities first.

e. Achieving something grand that for you is of great stature, such as writing a book, learning how to swim, learning how to ride a bike or learning to do something that was just a big accomplishment for you personally.

Keep the memory of these achievements within easy reach, to remind yourself always that once you had overcome something that was for you difficult, and that you had triumphed successfully. And for this reason, these achievements will also remind you that you can achieve anything – in all areas of your life – when you put your mind to it. Carry these like trophies on your wall – unless of course they are already trophies, indeed. And then you will have to find room for your next achievement.

## Never concern yourself about how other salespeople are doing.

Focus on yourself because you are in essence working for yourself. Focusing on another salesperson's performance and achievements will stop you from achieving your own goals. The best and safest way to think is to always wish the best for the other salesperson. If the other salesperson is making lots of sales, encourage them to make more. If they make ten sales for example, wish that it were twenty. Congratulating and encouraging them will rid you of the self-defeating pest named jealously.

❖

Positive thinking will inevitable solve at least half of all your problems!

# Topic 16

## POSITIVE THINKING CREATES SUCCESS WITH ANYTHING

*Think you can, think you can't; either way, you'll be right.*
*- Henry Ford*

There are only two ways a person can think when it comes to success – either negatively or positively. Not many options are there? Only two. Every negative thought has an equally positive one and every positive thought has an equally negative one. The difference between success and failure lies in the path of thinking you choose to follow.

It is easier to choose negative thinking over positive thinking because a little more effort and maturity is required on the latter. If you were to lose a well paying job – the lifeline of your survival – it would be very easy for you to wallow in pity and despair, which are just substitute words for negative thinking. The trick is to find something positive within the loss of that much needed job. Remember, for everything negative there is always a positive. The trick is to know what that positive is and how to connect with it.

Thus, a person who has lost his or her job may get a better job soon after if they remain positive. The universe will make it a positive experience for you *only* if you make it a positive experience for yourself. You will have the option to wallow in pity and give up or pull yourself together and *make* something good come out of nothing. The only way you are going to make that happen is to think positively.

There are many negative words in our vocabulary, but there are also an equal number of positive words in print and reality. Failure, despair, hunger, misery, fear, worry, hate, bad luck and no hope are just sub words that belong to the family of negative thinking. But there are other words, such as fun, happiness, peace, courage, strength, joy, riches, harmony, laughter and good luck that belong to the world of positive thinking, which can overcome the pathway that leads to destruction.

Negativity can and will be defeated in the world of positive thinking, but you must first accept and put yourself into that world of positive thinking. Positive thinking aims to defeat negativity, though negativity's thinking strives to do the same. It is nature's intention, however, that good should ultimately prevail over evil.

It should not be considered unrealistic to choose positive thinking as a norm simply because there are things to worry about. Why? Your positive way of thinking will create realistic solutions to things you are worrying about. Positive thinking is not a naïve or ignorant form of thinking. If you want to be successful in this life, it is the *only* form of thinking.

In Sales there are thousands of negative sub words that will try to defeat you, but be assured that the world of positive thinking is by your side to help you devour each and every one of the lies of negative thinking. Positive thinking will always be by your side to help you on the path to overcome all the tactics negative thinking has in store. You will ultimately succeed if you follow the path of positive thinking.

With anything in life – when it comes to success – there are only two ways of thinking. One is negative and the other is positive. Both are always competing to take control of you. If you are not careful then negativity will often, if not always, win. Be on your guard therefore and choose the ultimate choice of positive thinking, and your world will blossom. Positive thinking is your closest thing to heaven here on earth.

If you are not being successful in your Sales performance then you are doing something wrong; and that wrong has something to do with your way of thinking. And that way of thinking has something to do with negative thinking. And that thinking does not just have something to do with negative thinking, but *is* negative thinking itself. You should not whine when times become rough, but instead find the pathway that leads to positive thinking. This can be hard to find if you are already overwhelmed by the weeds of negativity.

Nevertheless, don't whine, but find a solution to every problem by implementing the method of positive thinking. Do this and you shall succeed. Success and positive thinking will blossom within you, hand in hand. Positive thinking will lead you down the road to successful living as you walk through this life here on earth.

# Topic 17

## GOOD LUCK AND YOU

*Luck always seems to be against the man who depends on it.*
        *- Anonymous*

*Good luck is often with the man who doesn't include it in his plans.*
        *- Anonymous*

Good luck is like age – it just sneaks up on you from seemingly nowhere. The biggest question good luck will tease you with is, do you feel lucky? Furthermore, do you act lucky? Do you think lucky? Do you talk lucky? If your answers to these questions are overwhelmingly "no," then that may be the reason why you haven't been experiencing good luck recently, or ever.

The greatest advice that good luck has for you is this: "Do not look for me. I will find you." Seeking good luck is wasting time that could have otherwise been used to do good deeds with.

You can create your own luck just like a cloud can create its own rain. You create your own luck by the way you act, think, feel, and talk. If these ingredients you're using to create your luck is distorted, then what will follow is bad luck all the way, like a thunderstorm. But if you're especially careful to watch how you think, then the sweet aroma of good luck will rain upon you almost everywhere you go.

Good luck is simply success finding you. Good luck will find those who work hard, like the sun rises upon the earth and makes it bright. Good luck is success, and success is the achievement of something desired – like a nice summer day.

Good luck is as bright as success is the color yellow. If you want to be lucky, then have brilliant thoughts. Turn every dark thought into a vivid horizon. Love bright thoughts like colors and then good luck will see you through the glare of the brilliant glow. Good luck cannot find you if your mind is in darkness. You must step out of the dark and come into the light so the sun may shine upon you.

## Good luck and positive thinking go hand in hand

You cannot have rain unless there are clouds. You cannot make omelets without breaking some eggs. You cannot be lucky without thinking positively. That is why positive thinking is so important towards achieving success. Positive thinking is also necessary to produce good body language and many more things. The things most people overlook are the main, fundamental things that could change their lives forever. Positive thinking is a guarantee to success. In order for good luck to make itself present onto you, the conditions must be right. And this condition is positive thinking. And what is positive thinking, you may ask?

Positive thinking is turning on the light to a dark day. Positive thinking is spending five minutes pondering what you can do to improve your situation rather than spending five hours thinking about all your misery. Positive thinking is forgetting the past unless you can pull something good out of it. Positive thinking means today is reality and now, and yesterday is gone forever. Let this day be the beginning of the rest of your life. Positive thinking is the oxygen you are inhaling right now – whether naturally or artificially – so that you can do whatever else is necessary to live strong. Positive thinking is a magnetic force that pulls you in the right direction on the pathway to success. Positive thinking is the smile on your face and the spark in your eye!

Positive thinking is the negative thoughts that comes into your head and are let out through the back door of your mind. Negative thoughts cannot survive in a room with bright lights, which does nothing but hurt their eyes. All they will see is an empty room, while bumping their heads against the walls.

It is important to know that negative thoughts will always try to enter your mind, but it is what you do with these negative thoughts that's important. You can set out a welcome mat for them and make the conditions just right for them, or you can turn up the pressure that forces them out of existence. The choice is a difficult one until you open your eyes and see the light. And when you see the light, then the choice will be a much easier one to look at.

*Therefore, if you're seeking to find good luck wherever you go, and with any situation that you must face, simply remember to use the two simple, yet powerful affirmations of:*

*"It's going to be good."*
*"If not, I'll make it good."*

*Thus, make good luck precede your path and clear the way in which you must walk.*

## Good luck is a magnetic force

You can attract good luck to you like a magnet if you can pull something good out of your bad luck. Everything that has a negative always has a positive aspect hidden somewhere in it as well. Once you learn the secret to uncovering the good within every bad situation, then you will have defeated bad luck. Every disappointment might just be a blessing.

Good luck is like a chain reaction. When you start receiving it, it keeps on coming towards you. It attaches itself to you like a lover gone wild. It will cleave to you like a breastplate. It will protect you fiercely from harm. Positive attracts positive as far as good luck is concerned, and as long as you remain positive good luck will pay you exceptional attention.

# Topic 18

---

# REGARD EVERY PROSPECT AS A GEM!

*Your luck is how you treat people.*
    *- Bridget O'Donnell*

In the hopes that your prospective buyer is not a rude, ignorant or disrespectful person, it is important to treat them as someone very special to you. Your love for your prospects should be so strong that not even rude ones will deter you. Love them all because some of them have made you who you are, and the rest of them will make you who you will be. So do not be prejudiced against any prospect and you will find out that they will not be prejudiced against you either.

Regard and treat every prospect as if they were the most important people in the world. Look into their eyes as if you were looking into the eyes of gold. See each of them as if they were the only person you've ever known. Position yourself to spend as much time as necessary with them. You do not want to *waste* any prospect. Try to get as much out of them – as when one squeezes water out of a leaf – so you can build a relationship that will grow into a tree.

If your prospect comes to your store, greet them with a warm welcome: "Thank you for coming to XYZ Company." If you are going to the prospect's home and they were not expecting you, introduce yourself with an apology: "I'm sorry to interrupt you." And if they were expecting you say, "Thank you for inviting me into your home."

Always greet everyone who is related to or with your prospect – especially if they are a part of the decision making process – which they usually are. As *soon* as you see someone with your prospect be quick to greet them with a smile and a "Hello, how are you?" If you hesitate, then you will be making a very big mistake – as the other person may take offense and feel the sense of being ignored. Even your prospect may be offended if you don't greet whomever else they're with.

Every prospect wants to be treated as if they are important. Every prospect wants to be treated like a king or queen; and don't forget the little princes and princesses too. So be sure and quick to treat them each like royalty. Roll out the purple carpet for them.

Acknowledge your prospect's children and shake their hands too, asking for their names and ages. Let them participate in the process of making a decision in purchasing the product or service.

You are the first *service* your prospect will experience with whatever it is you have to sell them. Therefore you must provide them with excellent service – that service being yourself. Give them a good first impression of your company by giving them a good first impression of yourself. Give them a taste of your product or service by giving them a taste of you. If they decide they like what you taste like, then most likely you've made yourself a sale.

## Listen To Them, And They Will Fall In Love With You!

Prospects love when you listen to them. They love the idea that someone is paying attention to them, hanging onto their every word. They love the idea of being acknowledged. You acknowledge your prospect by paying attention to them – by listening to them. It is very important to listen to what a prospect has to say to you even though it may not seem important. This is their test to see if you are really interested in them and are being sincere with them. If you pass the test, then you've just made yourself a new friend. Whatever you do, always be sure to listen to whatever your prospects are telling or saying to you.

But don't just listen to your prospects – participate in the discussion. Learn something new. Ask them follow up questions to let them know you're really listening. If you can, relate to what they're saying with something similar in your life.

Whatever you do, don't forget to treat each and every one of your prospects as someone special. Why? It will triple your Sale numbers! Treating others as we would like to be treated is the rule that we must learn to follow.

# Topic 19

---

## YOUR GOAL HAS EVERYTHING TO DO WITH YOUR SALES PERFORMANCE

*A journey of a thousand [miles] starts with the first step.*
  *- Lao Tzu*

*We must walk consciously only part way toward our goal, and then leap in the dark to our success.*
  *- Henry David Thoreau*

WARNING: If you do not have high goals – to make a lot of money, for example – then your profession should probably NOT be in Sales. You must be "hungry." But don't worry – this topic will help guide you in the right direction.

Ambition means you are aware that you can always do or be at least four times greater than who or what you currently are. That means that if you are making $30,000 per year then you could easily change that to a $120,000 dollar per year job by applying a little ambition. It means that if you are getting an 85 percent average on your tests, you could turn it into a 99.9 percent by applying a little ambition. Why not 100 percent, you may ask? Let's leave a little room for your doubt.

The achievements you will make as a salesperson will inevitably be determined by the goal you have set for yourself. If your goal is low or non-existent then your numbers will reflect that. If you goal is to exceed even your own goals, then your bank account will thank you for it! As a salesperson your job is to always aim high and try to make as much profit as you possibly can.

EVERY SALESPERSON MUST SET GOALS IF THEY EXPECT TO REACH THEIR NUMBERS, AND MAKE THE COMMISION THEY ARE LOOKING FOR. SET YOUR GOALS THESE WAYS:

✓ Establish a specific number of sales you're going to make each day. Write it down so that you won't forget your pledge. Always set your goal high, but always remain focused on making that *very first sale;* because without a first sale there is no possibility of making a second sale. Neither get or stay upset if you don't sell anything; instead, replace those feelings with a new and greater determination.

✓ *At the back of your mind* look at every prospect as a dollar sign ($), and be determined to get that dollar. Remember, the prospect looks at you as a product sign – for whatever product you're selling. That's why you're told to show your badge by managers – to identify yourself as the product.

✓ Be determined to reach your goal. Determination is a controlled rage that burns within you, which can be summed up as *enthusiasm with a cause.* Create an energy force within you and all around you. Deprive yourself of *want* until you get a sale. Tell yourself that you must and will sell today, everyday. Don't settle or make excuses. If food is your pleasure, then deprive yourself until you make a sale. If sex is your pleasure, then deprive yourself until you make your numbers. Be determined by depriving yourself of pleasure until your goal is met.

✓ Be focused. Your job is to get the prospect to say or express, "yes" to your offer, and like it. When things become a little hectic, overwhelming, frustrating or confusing simply remember, all you have to do is get that person to express, "yes." That's all. Always go back to the basics when more advanced techniques are not working for you. "Yes" is the key word and goal for all Sales endeavors.

When you're with a prospect, focus on that prospect only, for that period of time. Do not think about your previous customer and do not worry about your next customer either. Focus your time, energy

67

and thoughts only on the present prospect for now. Believe there is nothing else in the world except you, this prospect and their immediate surroundings – including their spouse, children, and whomever else or whatever else may be present. If you ignore this advice, then you will miss out on some potential opportunities and cues that could have been to your benefit. So when you're with a prospect, worry about nothing else – except any possible danger around you – this prospect and their surroundings are your sole concern for now.

## Be driven:

Be the salesperson who goes about his or her day as if they have no choice. Do it because it's the one thing you know and you do not know or want to know anything else because there's nothing else to know. Consider yourself as having no choice, so you put all your energy and effort into what you do. In this particular case burn your bridges and be focused on only moving forward.

❖

Do you know what separates a great salesperson from an average one? It is their desire to achieve. The measure of your desire to achieve will determine the measure of your paycheck at the end of the month. If your desire is lacking then your paycheck will be lacking as well. If your desire is long and infinite then you will store treasures upon the earth, and hopefully in heaven as well.

# Topic 20

---

## GET YOUR MIND INTO THE FLOW OF SALES BUSINESS

*I hardly recognize what I do well. I just do it.*
  *- Stephen Jay Gould*

Learn the method of warming up your mind before coming in contact with a prospect, just like when you warm up your car's engine during a cold morning breeze. Consider these few seconds or minutes before contact as precious. Be calm and at ease, and believe that everything is going to go well. Remember, there is always the calm before the storm – your enthusiasm being the storm. Therefore, focus on these three deeds when it comes to preparing your mind for a prospect:

✓ **Relax your body and mind.**
✓ **Always presume and expect that your prospect(s) is ready to buy.**
✓ **Ready yourself for their rejection.**

## 1) <u>Relax your mind and body</u>:

*Before coming in contact with a prospect, allow yourself to feel enthusiastic enough by doing something that lifts your spirit.* Listen to or sing a song you enjoy. Do or think about something that makes you feel good. Remember a joke.

A miserable salesperson is easily detected by their prospect(s); and your thoughts affect your body language. If you are contented or enthusiastic, then the prospect will feed off of that enthusiasm, which is contagious!

Breathe normally; relax your mind and body by inhaling deeply, holding it and letting go. Repeat this for about three to ten times periodically. A relaxed breathing pattern will help to ease your entire mind and body.

Don't think about or try to remember anything that you've learned at this point. Just relax your mind, and let things flow naturally.

## 2) <u>Always presume and expect that your prospect(s) is ready to buy</u>:

*Always believe that by some miraculous means each prospect is ready to buy.* Ignore the fact that your prospect may not buy today, by constantly presuming they will. Go with the presumption that each prospect you approach is going to give you the benefit of the doubt by purchasing your product. Present to them in a way that you're sure they're going to buy. Be confident and self-assured in your mind that what you have for them to claim is so great that anyone who does not take it is not in their right mind. Let your belief in the goodness of your product be contagious. Let it be that as soon as any prospect comes in contact with you, they catch the disease of your conviction. Let them feel, taste, smell, see, hear and know they must have it, and must have it now. Any other response from them is illogical, ridiculous, and not in the least bit funny.

## 3) <u>Ready yourself for their rejection</u>:

*Prepare yourself for each prospect's rejection.* Turn the prospect's rejection into a friendly challenge. Be on the alert for them saying, "No." Prepare yourself for the fact that they might not be interested. Then work your magic that will make them seriously consider or desire your offer and say, "Ok. Let's give it a try." You become a salesperson when you can sell something to someone who is not interested; not only to those who are prepared to buy.

After the prospect says, "No," try to strike up a conversation by asking them pointed questions. The longer you hold the prospect's attention, with a conversation, the more you will be able to insert your persuasive techniques into the conversation, and the more likely you will be able to ask them over and over again for the sale until they give in, and the more likely they will become interested in you and your product. Turn their rejection into a challenge for you to overcome.

Since most company's goal is to make their clients completely satisfied, ask the potential customer if they could give you the reason why they're not interested. Suggest that your manager has requested some feedback on how to improve the company's services. If a prospect is not interested, your main goal is to keep them talking so you can do whatever is necessary to change their mind.

❖

Bottom line: "*Be ready*" is the motto that every salesperson should use when dealing with any prospect!

# Topic 21

## RULES AND SUGGESTIONS THAT ALL SALESPEOPLE MUST LEARN TO FOLLOW

*Think like a man of action, act like a man of thought.*
  *- Henri Bergson*

*YOUR APPEARANCE IN FRONT OF A PROSPECT SHOULD BE NON-INTIMIDATING AND NON-DISTRACTING. USE THESE METHODS TO MAKE YOUR PROSPECT FEEL MORE AT EASE UPON FIRST SEEING YOU.*

**1) Consider** wearing light colored clothing, especially if your sales pertain to going to prospects' homes. This will psychologically help put their guard down. How often do you find a bank robber wearing beige pants with a bright yellow shirt? Believe it or not, pink seems to be the most non-threatening color to wear – even for men. Also the colors orange, red and light green will have a good effect.

**2) Avoid** wearing colognes or perfumes. In sales, it is better to be scentless. Any type of cologne or perfume – even the best smelling ones in the world – are most likely going to serve as a distraction between you and the prospect.

**3) Avoid** wearing glasses; consider contact lenses when you're doing your job as a salesperson. On a subconscious level, the glasses will be deemed as a barrier between you and the prospect. Prospects typically prefer to see your bare eyes without the barrier of glass.

Sometimes, however, glasses will actually enhance your credibility and make you seem more informative, but in general it will serve as a barrier

72

between you and your prospects. How often have you seen a politician wearing glasses on a regular basis before their electorate?

**4) Women:** Avoid wearing revealing outfits. Studies have shown that this serves more as a distraction and the invitation of other thoughts than it does towards increasing your sales output.

**5) Men:** Always strive to be clean shaven and avoid wearing a beard. The most successful salespeople in the world do not wear beards when it comes to sales; it's a turn off for prospects.

*THE PHYSICAL SPACE BETWEEN YOU AND THE PROSPECT IS A CRITICAL PART OF MAKING THE PROSPECT FEEL COMFORTABLE AND CONSEQUENTLY, YOUR ABILITY TO MAKE A SALE. CONTROL THE SPACE BETWEEN YOU AND THE PROSPECT THESE WAYS:*

**6) Upon** first meeting your prospect keep your distance at about four feet away. Everyone has a personal zone of space in which they become uncomfortable if someone enters it without permission. That personal space or distance is usually around four feet in the North American culture. In many Asian countries, for example, the personal zone will not be as great.

**7) As** you talk with a potential buyer, and as the relationship between both of you become friendlier, slowly move in closer towards them. Presuming you started your conversation about four feet away, move in gently about two feet closer. If you have something to show them then standing within one foot of each other would not be deemed as inappropriate.

**8) At** some point during your presentation try to position yourself below the prospect's eye level. For instance, if your prospect is short or shorter than you, it may prove beneficial to stoop down on one knee while demonstrating your product or service. This will make them feel "safe" with you. This will also give the prospect a sense that they're *in charge* of the situation. By nature, people like to *look down* on other people so they themselves may seem more important.

**9) When** negotiating price, attempt to position yourself as close as possible to the prospect. For instance, if you are sitting across the table during your presentation – when it's time for price negotiation – bring your chair over to their side. Be as close as possible, as when one comes close to another to comfort them. Why? You want the prospect to feel and know you are at their side, and that you understand them and their concerns. You want them to see that the relationship between both of you has grown into a more personal one. You want to be in control, and coming closer towards them at this point increases your position of control.

*ONE MUST FOLLOW CERTAIN RULES AS PART OF THE GENERAL SELLING PROCESS TO MAKE THINGS EASIER FOR THE PROSPECT'S COMPREHENSION AND YOUR OWN EASE OF MIND, AS A SALESPERSON.*

**10) If** you have more than one product or service to sell, focus on only one at a time. Introduce the most important product or service you believe the prospect is most likely to be interested in. Should they not be interested, then reveal the second item. If they are still not interested, then reveal the third, and so on. The bottom line: do not reveal a host of items all at the same time. You will only confuse both yourself and the prospect by doing that. It is much easier to handle a product or service one at a time.

**11) If** you do not know the answer to a prospect's question do not say, "I don't know," and leave it at that. Rather, say, "I'm not sure, but I'll be glad/happy to get that information for you." Furthermore, ask the prospect if there is anything else they would like to know before getting the answer for them. In any case it is important to continue selling and get all the answers for the prospect's questions *afterwards*. Be in control and not just an order taker.

**12) When** you're giving discounts to a prospect, keep in mind the 3% to 6% discount rule. What that means is, if your prospect is looking for a discount, give them a discount anywhere from 3 to 6 percent. For example, if you are offering your product or service at $100, then you can start from the 6 percent discount of $6 off. If your offer is $1,000, give them $60 off. If your offer is $10,000, give them $600 off.

Leave room to negotiate your offer about three times. And each time, discount your offer at around 3% to 6% from your current price offer.

Your discount itself should decrease a little bit more each time. For example, if you started your discount at 6 percent, then end your final offer at a 3 percent discount.

Let's call this *the 6 to 3 percent rule*, to make it easy to remember.

**13) Get** into the habit of thinking about and giving options to your prospect. For example, if they say they like red, ask them, "What's another option besides red that you like?" If they want a new item but can't afford it, ask them, "Would you consider a pre-owned item that's nearly new?" If they want to finance, ask them, "Have you ever considered a lease?" Then show them the benefits of a lease. If they want big then ask them if they would consider small. Then give them reasons why they should consider *small*.

Be in the habit of searching for and giving options to your prospects. Do not just settle on what they ask for. Sometimes they may not know what they really want. Your job is to mentally find and *suggest* options to your prospect and give them good reasons why. The bottom line: If plan A does not work out you'll have plan B next in line to work with. Always open up your prospect's mind to options.

**14) Be** in the habit of answering a prospect's questions with questions of your own. For example, if a prospect asks you a question such as, "How much is it?" ask them, "How much were you looking to spend?" If they ask, "Do you have them in another color besides blue?" you may ask, "Don't you like blue?" Bottom line, find out the reason why a prospect may be asking you a particular question. Try to get into their head to understand what exactly they are looking for or are *not* looking for.

*YOU ARE RESPONSIBLE FOR ALL YOUR ACTIONS AND THE WAY YOU HANDLE BUSINESS AS A SALESPERSON. BE SURE TO HANDLE BUSINESS THE RIGHT WAY THAT WILL BENEFIT YOU IN THE LONG RUN.*

**15) A** serious salesperson will be an organized salesperson: Organize your material for prospects and customers in binders and folders; and label them appropriately to make them easier to access.

**16) Always** remember to make follow up phone calls to both prospects and your current customers. If you didn't sell your prospect on the first contact, be sure to call them back or go back to them in person to close the sale.

**17) Always** call your most recent customers one day after the sale to make sure they're happy. Then call again one week later, and then three weeks later. You may want to then send them a post card every six months to find out if all is well.

**18) In** the process of fishing for customers – prospecting – be sure to leave your mark wherever you go, meaning, anywhere you go strive to leave a card with your name and number, along with your service. Even more emphatic, strive to leave flyers of what you do wherever possible.

**19) Never** assume anything, unless it's the assumption that every prospect is going to buy from you. Always ask the questions that should be asked and do the things that need to be done.

**20) Remember** that rules were meant to be broken, sometimes. Think out of the box to match your current conditions if your knowledge of the rules of Sales isn't currently working. But be prepared for the consequences that an independent mind brings.

❖

Be sure to use these rules and suggestions when selling products and services to prospects (Obey these laws.) They will make your life much easier, advancing you in the great lifestyle of a successful salesperson.

# Topic 22

---

## POWERFUL SALES WORDS TO REMEMBER

*If you can teach me a new word, I'll walk all the way to China to get it.*
*- Turkish proverb*

Certain *power words* can increase your chances of making an impact and/or a new awareness in a prospect's mind. They can therefore also help to make a sale. Strive to memorize and use these distinctive, successful power words and phrases. Strive to make these distinctive key words a part of your everyday Sales pitch when you're presenting in front of any prospect; and in dealing with their objections.

### Twelve Very Powerful Sales Words:

At first the sales words below may not seem very appealing as living up to being power words that persuade others; but after you comprehend how they work you should be persuaded otherwise.

| | | |
|---|---|---|
| You | Money | Guarantee(d) |
| Because | Health(y) | By |
| So | Or | If |
| Very | Jack/Jill | When |

*You.* *You* is a very personal word because it is specifically speaking or directing the attention to *You*. *You* are important. This is done for *you*. *You* are the reason I'm here. This is all for *you*. When communicating with a potential buyer it is always wise to personalize the sale by making the main subject of your topic *you*, the prospect. *You* is perhaps the most powerful pronoun that can be used with any prospect.

***Because:*** The question a prospect asks themselves is "why" should they buy from you. Every question that starts with *why* should always be answered with the word *because*. Every question asking "why" should always have a reason explaining *why* it is so.

Prospects and people in general appear to be genetically inclined to take heed of the word *because*. It is a mystery word that seems to speak for itself. If you use the word *because* as a reason for what you're doing, you'll actually increase the possibility of getting an agreement just by using this word. "Give me a drink *because* I'm thirsty," is twice as powerful than just, "Give me a drink." "Follow me this way *because* I have something to show you," is much more powerful than just, "Follow me."

***So:*** The word *so* explains to the prospect how they will benefit from what you're selling them. "You will have access to a more reliable and safer banking system *so* you won't have to worry about your money being stolen. The word *so* explains the logic behind anything when it is used *correctly*. It lets the prospect know what's in it for them by connecting the word *so* in your benefit statement.

***Very:*** The word *very* strongly emphasizes the importance and the greatness of what you have to offer. This adjective enhances anything – any noun or other adjective – that follows. "You are *very* beautiful." "I can see that you are *very* intelligent."

***Money:*** As long as your presentation has something to do with the prospect saving or not losing money, that is a major factor that will whet their appetite. Prospects like the idea of the game of saving money or reducing their cost. Even if your product may be more expensive than what the prospect was looking for, you could still show them that you are saving them money on a value basis. Expensive things cost lots of money because they are worth lots of money. And expensive things that cost lots of money hold a lot of value because they can be resold for lots of money. So in that sense, you would still be saving the prospect money in the long run.

*Health(y):* Most people are concerned with their *health,* and those who aren't, should be. Providing a service that claims to be of benefit to the prospect's *health* is music to their ears. A product that will reduce their stress and worry would provoke them to act if they believe the stated claim. It is not only herbs and medicines and medical equipment that can be used to provide *health* to customers. Almost any type of product can improve a prospect's *health* just by the possibility, for example, that it would save them money. Money earned is stress reduced in the mind of an intuitive prospect. Try to tailor your presentation in such a way that it will improve the *health* and reduce the stress of the prospect if they purchase your proposal.

*Or* : Use the word *or* to give the prospect a choice or an option between two things that are basically equivalent. "Are you going to take this home now *or* is 4:00pm today better?" "Do you want to write your phone number down or would you prefer to just whisper it in my ear?"

Usually, the use of the word *or* is used to separate two completely different options, but in sales you can use it to your advantage by connecting the same goal in a different way. This word will make the prospect think they are being given a choice while in fact, they are being giving an option that will provide you with the same essential result.

*Jack/Jill:* The sweetest and most wonderful sound to any person's ears and the best word to someone's eyes is their own name. If used politely, the sound of their name coming from another person can instantly give them a warm, fuzzy feeling all over. When you've just met someone try to get their name as soon as possible, within the first 5 to 40 seconds if possible, and use it back to them immediately. "Jill, it's nice to meet you. I'm Ken, by the way." Shake hands. "So Jill, tell me…" Don't overuse their name though – you may wear it out. Use it in a natural and unforced manner.

*Guarantee(d):* A *guarantee* assures the prospect that they won't have anything to worry about. It tells them that they won't regret it. It lets them know they can trust whatever you're telling them is the truth and that you can back it up with facts.

**By:** This word shares the same exact sound effect as the word "buy." The good news for you as a salesperson is you can use this word as the preposition that it is, and the prospect's subconscious mind will hear it as the verb "buy", as in "buy now."

Repeatedly using the word *by* will eventually sink into the prospect's subconscious mind. For example: *By* the way, do you like red or yellow? I'll have this ready for you *by* 5 p.m. *By* having our services you'll have a trouble free experience .By taking this offer you'll be saving yourself a lot of money. *By* what you're saying I understand where you're coming from. *By* trying our services you'll get the first month risk free. You can come *by* me a little closer. Just *by* listening to what you're saying, I can understand how you feel.

When selling, try to use the word *by* as much as possible – about ten to thirty times should prove effective. This word is interpreted by the subconscious mind to mean "buy," as in, "Buy this service today."

**If :** Use the word *if* as a question to determine the prospect's mindset and to determine if you're going in the right direction. Examples: "If you had the money to buy a computer today, would this be the one, Ms. Jill?" "If I could save you up to $1,000 per year, how would you feel about that?" "If the numbers are right, will you take the car home today?"

**When:** The word *when* can be used to make the assumption that the prospect is ready or is getting ready to buy your product or service. Examples: "When we install the TV here, will you have a bigger table for it by then? "When can we set up an appointment for you?" The word *when* can be used to make the assumption that X has already happened or it's only a matter of time before X will be put into effect. It presumes that it's not a matter of if but *when*.

❖

## Words to *AVOID* Using in your Sales Presentations

There are many words you should *avoid* when presenting your products or services. Some are more obvious than others. Below is a list of some of the more difficult to detect words that may creep into your presentations. Avoid these words.

***But***: Prospects hate to be wrong, though they frequently are. Even if a prospect is flat out wrong you must restrain the manner in which you correct them. Even if you were to agree with a prospect and then use the word *but*, you are actually saying that everything before that *but* is invalid.

Use the word *and* or nothing if need be, to correct a prospect who's ideas are incorrect. "I understand what you are saying Mr. Fitzpatrick, *and* if I could show you exactly what I'm talking about, I'm sure we'll be able to come to an agreement."

***Estimate***: When you tell a prospect you are going to give them an "*estimate*" of cost, etc., you are actually telling them they can think about it and come back later. Using the word *estimate* takes away the urgency to buy now. Try to avoid this word.

***Don't***: Avoid using the word *don't* and its associates when advising someone not to do something. "Don't believe that I'm here to rob you," will make the prospect feel inclined to do the opposite of what the statement said. All they'll have to do is remove the word *don't*, and there you have it: "Believe that I'm here to rob you." Placing *don't* at the beginning of a sentence stirs the prospect's disobedient nature. "Don't believe that guy who told you his service is better," turns into, "Believe that guy who told you his service is better." Avoid starting a sentence with the word *don't*, even though some of my writing is guilty of using it.

***I/Me/My/Mine***: As much as possible, avoid putting yourself and your interests first when it comes to providing for your prospect. People are selfish by nature and all they want to know is what's in it for them. Put your prospect first and only be concerned about caring for their needs. Give them the stage. Let it be all about them and what you can do for them. Your prospect wants to hear the word *you*, referring to them, rather than the word *I*, referring to you the salesperson.

***It's Not My Fault*:** Prospects don't want to hear that it's not your fault. They don't care whose fault it is. All they want is the problem fixed. And as far as they're concerned, it is your fault until the problem gets fixed. Instead try saying, "I apologize for the inconvenience. I'll do my best to correct the situation as soon as possible."

***Contract*:** Prospects hate to be tied into something they must commit to. The word *contract* conjures up the idea that they are stuck in a deal they may not have wanted to be a part of in the first place. Turn the word *contract* into the word *agreement*. The word *agreement* in place of *contract* is much more user friendly.

***Sign*:** When asking a prospect to put their signature on a piece of paper it gives them the uneasy feeling that they are signing their life or privacy away. To prevent that feeling use a warmer phrase such as, "I need your autograph right here for me, please."

***Honestly*:** This word is more obvious than the rest, in that it creates a bad taste in the mouths of those who hear it. If a person uses the word *honestly* then most likely what they are about to tell you is a lie. It could also mean that what they just said before the word *honestly* was a lie. Delete this word from your sales vocabulary.

***Buy*:** The word *buy* is definitely not a word of endearment to the ears of a prospect. It's a nuisance and a pressure button that turns them off. Instead of using the word *buy*, replace it with the friendlier and more courteous word *claim*. "*Claim* our offer today and you will get a $20 discount!"

Even though using the word *by* subconsciously persuades prospects to buy, ironically the word *buy* itself is actually considered a turn off. Unlike the word *by*, *buy* does not speak to the subconscious mind, but rather to the prospect's conscious and resistant mind, which is prone to be turned off by this familiar sales word. The bottom line is that *by* speaks to the subconscious or non-resistant mind, while *buy* speaks to the conscious or resistant mind.

**Interested:** Never ask a prospect if they are *interested* because they are not. It is your job to make them interested. If you have done your job then you don't need to ask them if they are interested. You are supposed to make them interested and assume the sale.

**Just:** Requesting a prospect to give you *just five* minutes to show them something is degrading your service or product. A prospect is not *just* looking for something to be shoved down their throats, and by using the word *just* does not help the situation. Delete the word *just* from your vocabulary when you are trying to get a prospect to look at what you have. Simple say, "If you give me five minutes of your time I'll show you what I have."

**Help:** Asking a prospect, "Can I *help* you?" or "How can I *help* you?" is ridiculous. You are not in the business of helping people – doctors are. Your job is to persuade prospects you have something they want or need, or that you are going to make them want or need – and they know it.
Though on many occasions you will be technically helping your prospects, don't use this word with them. Instead, say, "How may I *assist* you?" or "How may I be of *service* to you?"

❖

## More Power Words And Phrases To Use In Your Vocabulary:

Anyone who wants to advertise anything, either in person or in print, will be successful if they mix and match the applicable words and phrases below. These power words will be a treasure trove to those who know how to use them well. Again, these words and phrases can be used for any type of sales, advertisement or marketing endeavor, whether, orally or in writing.

---

ACCOMMODATING

APPROVED

ASSURE

ATTACHMENT

ATTRACTIVE

BARGAIN

BEAUTIFUL

BECOME A MEMBER

BELIEVE

BENEFIT(IAL)

BEST

BETTER

BOTH

BOTTOM LINE

CARE

CERTAIN

COLOR(FUL)

COMPARE

COMPETITIVE

COMPLETE

CONFIDENT(IAL)

CONGRATULATIONS!

CONNECTION

CONVENIENT

DEFINITELY

DELIVER(ED)

DIRECTLY

DISCOUNT(S)

DISCOVER

DON'T WORRY

EASILY

ENCOURAGE

ENDORSED

ENHANCE(D)

EXACT(LY)

EXCELLENT (CUSTOMER)

EXCITING

EXCLUSIVE

EXPERIENCE(D)

EXTRA

FAIR

FAST(EST)

FAVORITE

FEEDBACK FROM YOU

FEW

FIRST COME, FIRST SERVED

FIT

FOCUS

FOR ME

FOR YOU

FOR YOUR CONVENIENCE

FREE

FRIENDLY

GAIN

GENUINE

GET A FEEL FOR

GIVE IT A TRY

GIVE YOU

GOOD CHOICE

GRAB A HOLD OF

GREATEST

HAPPY

HELPFUL

HOW DO YOU FEEL ABOUT?

HOW HAS OUR SERVICE BEEN?

HOW WOULD YOU LIKE TO?

HOWEVER

HOW TO

HURRY

I AGREE WITH YOU

I APOLOGIZE FOR THE INCONVENIENCE

I UNDERSTAND

I'LL TRY MY BEST

IF YOU, THEN

IMAGINE

IMMEDIATE(LY)

IMPORTANT

IMPRESSIVE

IMPROVE(D)

INCLUDED

INTELLIGENT DECISION

INTRODUCING

INVITE YOU

IT COMES WITH

IT'S HERE

JOIN

JUST ARRIVED

KEEP

LATEST

LET'S DO THIS

LIFETIME

LIKE

LIMITED (TIME OFFER)

LONG LASTING

LOTS OF FUN

LOVE

LOWEST

LUXURY

MADE JUST FOR YOU

MAGICAL

MAKE

MORE

NATURAL

NEW

NOTED

NOW

ONLY FOR YOU

OPPORTUNITY

OPTION(S)

ORIGINAL

OUTSTANDING

PARTICIPATE

PERSONAL(IZED)

PLEASANT

PLEASE

POPULAR

POWERFUL

PROFESSIONAL

PROFIT(ABLE)

PROMISE

PROMISE ME THAT YOU WILL

PROUD

PROVE(N)

QUICK AND EASY

QUICK(LY)

RARE

REAL

RECOMMEND(ED)

REDUCE(D)

REFUND(ABLE)

RELAX(ING)

RELIABLE

RESULT(S)

REVEAL(ING)

REWARD

SAFE(TY)

SALE

SAMPLE

SATISFACTION

SATISFY

SAVE

SCARCE

SECRET(S)

SECURE

SECURITY

SEE FOR YOURSELF

SEE WHY

SELECTED

SHARE

SHOW YOU

SIMPLIFIED

SMART

SMOOTH TRANSITION

SO THAT YOU MAY GET A TASTE OF

SOPHISTICATED

SPECIAL (OFFER)

SPECIFIC

STATE-OF-THE-ART

STRONG

STRONGLY RECOMMEND(ED)

STURDY

STYLE

SUCCESSFUL

SUITABLE (FOR YOU)

SURE

SURPRISE

TAKE ADVANTAGE OF

TEAM

TEST DRIVE

TESTED

THANK YOU

THAT YOU MAY NOT BE AWARE OF

THIS IS WHAT I CAN/WILL DO FOR YOU

THOUGHTFUL

TO COMPLIMENT YOUR HOME WITH

TO SATISFY YOUR NEEDS

TODAY

TOGETHER

TOUGH

UNCONDITIONAL

UNIQUE

UNSURPASSED

UNUSUAL

URGENT

USEFUL

VALUABLE

WE

WE WOULD LIKE TO EARN YOUR BUSINESS

WE DON'T WANT TO LOSE YOU

WE'LL WAIVE

WE'VE NEVER MET

WELCOME TO

WERE YOU AWARE?

WHAT I CAN DO FOR YOU IS

WHAT WE'LL DO IS

WHEN WAS THE LAST TIME?

WITH YOU

WONDERFUL

WOULD/DO YOU MIND IF

YES

YOU AND I

YOU DESERVE

YOU QUALIFY

YOU WILL

YOU WON'T HAVE TO WORRY ABOUT

YOU'RE ENTITLED

YOU'RE RIGHT

❖

Many times you will find that it's not what you say, but how you *word* or *phrase* it that will determine the sale. One single word can make a big difference as to whether or not a prospect is going to buy from you. Thus, choose your words and phrases with care.

# Topic 23

---

# TAKE CONTROL OF THE SITUATION

*He who reigns within himself, and rules passions, desires, and fears, is more than a king.*
*- John Milton*

What is the best way to take control of a sales situation between you and the prospect? The best way is to make the prospect feel as if they are the one in control. How would you go about doing this? You start by sounding as if you are making requests as opposed to telling them what to do. For instance you would say, "Could you come closer, please?" as opposed to saying, "Come closer." Another great way of making requests is: *If you could just X, please*, as in, "If you could just come closer, please!" Even one word can make a difference in the perception of a prospect's mind who wants to be in control.

And again, "Follow me this way," is a totally different command than just saying, "Follow me." In "Follow me this way," the main point is not asking the prospect to follow you, but *where* to follow you because the fact that they *will* follow you is already presumed to have been established. "Can I talk to you for a few minutes?" is totally different than, "Can I talk to you?" Why? The fact that you added on, "for a few minutes," makes the subject not if you can talk to them, but for how long. So when making commands, be sure to follow up with a statement that suggests not *if* they will, but *how* they will, *when* they will, *where* they will or *why* they will.

When you are in control your aim is simply to get the prospect to do what you want them to do, without having them feel uneasy about doing it. The way you phrase it will determine the mood of whether or not the prospect will feel comfortable about doing it.

Taking control boils down to making the prospect do what you want them to do. For instance, if you want the prospect to let you into their home you'll say, "If you could just let me in please, I can show you X!"

and expect that they will say, "Yes." Another way is to ask the prospect to follow you and they comply, or to come closer to you, from behind a storm door, for example. "Could you just step outside, please?" or "If you could just step outside, please!" Think of it as if you are a police officer directing what you want the prospect to do.

Be forceful but gentle. Be as forceful as a gentle breeze. Tell your prospect what they need rather than asking them if they need it. Let yourself into the prospect's heart with subtlety, rather than waiting for them to allow you in unsubtly. Make your presence known rather than hoping that it will be shown. Mentally pull the prospect towards you and push them into action, as opposed to them pulling you forward just to push you away. Stimulate their curiosity to say, "yes."

If they're not sure, reassure them that they won't regret it because everyone else is doing it and loving it. Whatever the case may be, if you detect weakness from the prospect, exhibit your mental strength to overcome the objection. Every prospect has a weak point – it is up to you to know what it is and to transform their weakness into a strong sale.

*Fact: It is important to note that most prospects will grant your request if it is reasonably stated and spoken with assertiveness.*

## The way you say it, and other things that influence the prospect:

Your tone of voice is a key influence in determining how a prospect will respond to your request. It may be as important as the request itself in the eyes of the prospect. A weak tone will achieve little success, if any. It is important to note that when making a request, your tone of voice must be assertive and your words clearly stated. Your voice must be absent of doubt and uncertainty. Your demeanor must also be one of expectation that your request will be fulfilled. If you want to be in control your approach must not be weak. You should be confident *enough* so the prospect may feel safe or satisfied enough putting their faith in you, yet all along still thinking that they are in control.

❖

Often, it's not what you say, but how you say it that will determine your success.

# Topic 24

---

## THREE VERY PERSUASIVE SALES TECHNIQUES TO KNOW

*Be sure you put your feet in the right place, then stand firm.*
  *- Abraham Lincoln*

Here are three exciting, persuasive techniques that when mastered, can produce amazing results:

> **1. Verbal Pacing and Leading**
> **2. Anchoring**
> **3. Binding**

## 1) VERBAL PACING AND LEADING

*Verbal Pacing* is stating things that are facts in general or that are generally believed to be facts and which are widely known. *Leading* is stating something you want to come across as being fact, though it has not been officially proven. An effective presentation of a pace and lead will usually start with three paces and one lead:

> Pace    Pace    Pace    Lead

**Here are three examples:**

a.　Pace:　　　　Everybody wants to get the best for less.
　　Pace:　　　　Prices for certain products and services have been going up steadily each decade.
　　Pace:　　　　You can buy a product for half as much depending on where you shop.

　　Lead:　　　　Our services will give you the best value for your money.

❖

b.    Pace:            Diabetes is the silent killer.
       Pace:            Many people with this disease don't know it.
       Pace:            This disease can even cause blindness if not monitored.

       Lead:            Our herbal tea will help regulate your blood-sugar levels to prevent you from developing diabetes.

❖

c.    Pace:            Safety and reliability are very important factors when choosing a car.
       Pace:            There is an accident every four seconds in the United Stated, according to the most recent census.
       Pace:            The government recommends that all vehicles should have side airbags along with front airbags.

       Lead:            The safety features and reliability factors of this vehicle is one of the best on the market currently.

Finding a pace routine that fits into your presentation can be a challenging one. It is recommended that you do some research before hand and train yourself to pace and lead as it applies to your product or service.

A salesperson who has a grip on pacing and leading will follow a chart like this:

| | | | |
|------|------|------|------|
| Pace | Pace | Pace | Lead |
| Pace | Pace | Lead | Lead |
| Pace | Lead | Lead | Lead |
| Lead | Lead | Lead | Lead |

## 2) ANCHORING

An anchor is a method used to make someone recall pleasant memories, and then associate those pleasant memories to what you're offering. A person can recall a pleasant experience by a certain smell, a certain touch, a certain sight, a certain taste or a certain sound. There are other ways too.

You can summon your prospect to remember a pleasant feeling they once experienced by using certain anchoring methods. For instance, you could summon a pleasant feeling within a prospect by asking them, "How did you feel when you first learned to balance and ride a bike without falling?" or "How did you feel the first time you went out on a date with someone you really liked?" Then you could create an association anchor by tapping on your product and suggesting to the prospect that they will experience the same good feeling when they claim your product.

**Other examples of anchoring:**

Ask your prospect,
"How did it feel the first time you kissed someone you really liked?"
(When they answer, associate that feeling with what you're selling.)
"When was the last time someone made you laugh your socks off?"
"What is the feeling you get when you're eating your favorite ice-cream?"
"How do you know when you really like someone?"
"What was the most fun you had this year?"
"What makes you feel really good?"
"What makes you happy?"
"What makes you laugh?"
"What's your favorite food?"
"What's your favorite drink?"
"What turns you on?"
"How does loving someone feel for you?"
"Can you remember a time when you were doing something that was so much fun you didn't want to stop?"

When the prospect gives you an honest answer – which they should – then tailor your presentation to suggest that your offer will create those same feelings within them. Subtly put your proposal in view as the prospect recalls these pleasant memories. This should make their subconscious mind associate those pleasant feelings with your product or service.

## 3) <u>BINDING</u>

Binding is a process of bringing two or more things together to produce an effect. The word "or" is the most common way to create bindings.

Using the word "or" usually indicates that you are going to give an option of two different scenarios. The trick to using this method to persuade is to connect bindings that are one in the same, but stated using different words. The end result is intended to be basically the same.

**Binding examples:**

"Do you want me to drop this off at your house later or are you going to take it home now?" The bottom line is that it's going to be at their home one way or another.

"Which is good for you, Tuesday at 3 pm or Saturday at 2:30pm?" The bottom line is that one of these days is going to be good for them instead of never.

"Which one would you like to take home today, the red or blue one?" The bottom line is that they're taking home one today. It doesn't matter to you which color it is.

❖

Sales should be fun, so have fun trying these techniques.

# Topic 25

## HYPNOTIC TECHNIQUES ON HOW TO PERSUADE ALL PEOPLE!

*Confusing a targeted audience is one of the necessary ingredients for effective mind control.*
  *- Joost Meerloo*

Hypnosis is the process of tapping into an individual's, or as they say it in hypnosis, a *subject's* subconscious mind, by quieting that individual's conscious mind. The purpose of hypnosis is to be in direct contact with the individual's subconscious mind in order to embed commands or what is known as *suggestions* during hypnosis.

This topic delves into the method of covert hypnosis as a way to persuade others. If you are not comfortable with this form of persuasion it is not necessary to use it as a part of selling. But for your education it would be wise to know this method because some people will apply it on you. Therefore, you will have a better chance to protect yourself when you observe this technique being used.

Hypnotic techniques are a form of commanding the subconscious mind of the prospect, in order to get them to do what you want them to do. Four ways to apply hypnotic techniques are to: 1) Confuse the prospect by asking them questions, or by making statements, that do not make any sense, 2) Implying to the prospect that the more they disagree with you will actually make them agree more, 3) Using repetition as a way to wear down the prospect's resistance and 4) Using hypnotic words and phrases that speak directly to the prospect's subconscious level.

## a)     Confusing the prospect by asking questions or by making statements that don't make any sense

This covert form of command is intended to confuse the prospect's mind into searching for an answer to a question or a statement that just does not make any sense. The aim is for you to answer the prospect's question while they are still searching for the meaning of what you said. The hope is that by giving them an answer to a question that does not make any sense, they are prone to agree with you. Lawyers and other professions often use this technique. Here are some examples of questions and statements meant to confuse the prospect:

If you expected me to believe that, you wouldn't have said that.

Your reasoning lets me know what you're unaware of.

Do you believe what you knew you thought?

Are you unaware of what you forgot?

Why are you trying to convince yourself of what you already know?

Do you really believe what you had known?

If you didn't want me to stick around, then I would not have been gone a long time ago.

While the subject/prospect is still searching for the meaning to what you said, then make a suggestion/statement that you want them to obey/follow: "Just take my advice, and buy this product, and you'll be alright."

❖

This technique should only be used by those who are comfortable using it, as it may be deemed too sneaky a tactic for the average person who wants to feel dignified in their profession. If you don't feel comfortable with it, then don't use it.

However this method can be used for good to the unruly, or for people who are stubborn about doing what they need to do. By using this method you will be confusing their stubbornness. And that confusion will loosen the grip to their stubborn thinking and make them act in a more appropriate manner.

❖

**b)  Implying to the prospect that the more they disagree with you will actually make them agree more**

This form of covert hypnosis is a little more user friendly than the latter. It aims to use the prospect's resistance against them. It confuses them slightly while convincing the prospect that what they are saying or thinking is the total opposite to what they had intended. It's a technique that tries to convince the prospect that what they think they want is actually the opposite of what they truly want. It uses the prospect's words and thoughts against them in a reverse effect. Examples:

> The more you X, the more you will X
> The more you X, the less you will X
> The less you X, the less you will X
> The less you X, the more you will X
> The more you X, the better you X
> The less you X, the better you X

✓ The more you disagree, the more interested you'll become with what I'm saying.

✓ The more you're not interested, the more you'll find yourself intrigued with what I'm saying.

✓ The more you say no, the more you'll find yourself agreeing with everything I say, and the more you agree, the more you want it. And the more you want it, the better you'll feel.

✓ The less time you have to listen, the more you'll understand everything I have to say. And the more you understand, the more you will want to hear it!

✓ The more you listen and do what I say, the better you will feel doing it!

❖

## c) Using repetition as a way to wear down the prospect's resistance

Repetition of words is a form of hypnosis in itself. In fact, the whole theory of hypnosis is based on repetition of words and acts. The aim of repetition is to turn the prospect's mind into a daze so that they will find it hard to stay alert and conscious.

Repetition is the key that turns your prospect's subconscious buying mode ON.

You should not expect to say a bunch of magic words once, and then see results. You must be continuous and repetitious until the person's subconscious mind gets the message. Four to seven various tries or of saying the same exact words should do the magic trick if it is meant to be.

In real hypnosis, using repetitious words and deeds 100 times would be a typical session to induce someone into hypnosis. The bottom line: Be repetitious if you plan to embed your hypnotic commands into the prospects subconscious mind: "Claim it now!" "Take it home today!" "Autograph here!" "It's yours!" "You know you want it!" "Claim it now!"

❖

## d) Using hypnotic words and phrases that speak directly to the prospect's subconscious level

Hypnotic words and phrases are simply a tried and tested collection of words or phrases put together in order to tap into the prospect's subconscious mind more influentially. The purpose is to obtain easy access to the prospect's subconscious mind by allowing them to follow the commands of your subtle hypnotic words. Here are some examples of words that could potentially be used to tap into the prospect's subconscious mind:

**You will...**
Examples:
- ✓ You will feel more comfortable when you actually sit in that seat.
- ✓ You will fall asleep after I'm done reading this book to you.
- ✓ You will enjoy listening to what I have to say.

**When you...**
Examples:
- ✓ When you buy this product, you will love it.
- ✓ When you do as I told you, you will understand exactly what I was talking about.
- ✓ When you behave yourself, I will give it back to you.

**As you...**
Examples:
- ✓ As you follow my instructions, you'll find the job much easier to accomplish!
- ✓ As you see, you'll be saving yourself a lot of money today by switching over to our service!
- ✓ As you know, rum and raisin ice cream tastes better than vanilla ice cream.

**Just imagine...**
Examples:
- ✓ Just imagine yourself driving home in this new car today!
- ✓ Just imagine sleeping on this soft, big bed tonight!
- ✓ Just imagine we were out on a date with each other!

As you may have noticed from the above examples, you can mix and match these hypnotic words into one sentence. In other words, multiple commands can be used at the same time.

There are many more hypnotic commands, but these were provided because they are more likely the ones that you will find convenient to remember and use.

❖

Some, if not all, of these hypnotic techniques are common techniques that people who are trying to convince others use everyday, anyway. But they may not know it creates a subtle form of hypnosis to their recipient. But you know. And you now know what you ought to do, and how. And if someone should try any of these techniques on you, you will have a firmer grip on things and know how to handle them directly, right?

# Topic 26

## BODY LANGUAGE: THE LANGUAGE THAT WILL GENERATE THE MOST SALES

*The man who speaks the truth is always at ease.*
  *- Persian proverb*

The most important thing to know about body language is that your body language is controlled by the way you think. If you think negatively then your body language will reflect that. Conversely, if you think positively then your body language will be welcoming and friendly. Thus, if you want to use your body language to influence others you will have to adapt your whole thinking structure to that of wanting to influence others.

The first thing most people see is your facial expression and your overall body language. This language tells them within a second or two whether or not they will want to deal with you. A negative form of body language can turn a person off immediately – sometimes before that person even sees you. Your negative vibe will travel through the air just like cellular phone signals are transmitted invisibly over the airwaves.

Body language is the overall expression of your body movements and gestures. It could be a conscious movement or a subconscious one depending on how aware you are of your body at any given time. You can manipulate your body language to work for you and persuade others to do what you desire. This form of persuasion is called persuasion through non-verbal communication.

The scientific term for body language is *kinesis*. Studies from the 1970's have found that about 55% of your overall body language determines whether or not a prospect will buy from you. And more recent studies have shown that this percentage can reach as high as 70 to 80%.

Therefore it is important to know how to communicate to prospects non-verbally in order to increase your sales output.

## The Way You Think Influences Your Body Language:

If you don't remember anything else here concerning body language, remember one thing: Your body language is developed by the way you think. For example, if you have tense or anxious thoughts then your body language will be uptight. If you have open, warm thoughts then your body language will reflect an open and warm appearance. So the place to start exhibiting influential body language is with your thoughts. Develop thoughts that are open and kind, and lose the uptightness, and this will transform the language of your body so others can warm up to you and be persuaded by you and your charm.

## The Space Around You:

Along with your body language there is an invisible aura that each of us carries. This aura contains the energy of our thoughts even more so than our body language. For example, if you are thinking angry thoughts, an invisible aura of steam and distress will surround you, and others will pick up on your aura even though it can't be seen. Your invisible aura travels through air like atoms float within the atmosphere. It's there even though you can't see it. That is why once again, it is imperative that you maintain positive thoughts. Only positive thoughts will be able to redefine you from the sparks of a negative aura that turn prospects off.

❖

There are many body language positions you can learn and practice in order to make your prospects feel at ease with you. Since at the time of this writing no official names have been given to these different positions, we shall consider general terms. Following is a list of some of the most popular forms of kinesis you can experiment with:

**Open, Friendly Body Language:** Think open and friendly thoughts and your body will reflect this to the people who surround you. Be like a door with a welcome mat that says, "Come on in." Be friendly and approachable with your thoughts and your body language will mirror those thoughts exactly. Be ready to shake the nearest hand in front of you. Position yourself this way and it will increase your ability to obtain the open and friendly body language.

**Docile, Inquisitive Body Language:** This body language is one of wanting to learn and assumes a humble, attentive position. Do not cross your arms and don't put your hands in your pockets. Your shoulders will slump forward a little to hear what is being said so you can follow along and pay full attention to what you are listening to. A look of wonderment will be on your face, with a subtle type of innocence. With this body language you are open to take in what is being taught to you without the rush to judgment or defensiveness. You will be a good student of learning.

**Smiling, Colorful Body Language:** A smile is the safest facial expression and avoids any misunderstandings. As long as your smile is sincere and seemingly effortless then you will have achieved your goal in letting prospects warm up to you quickly. You can never go wrong with a smile, but a frown is always questionable. It only takes seven muscles to smile but over forty to make a frown. Smile for everyone and your face will be like a warm summer day shining upon them.

A serious looking face is not cool in the real world. Only in those action movies does a frown stand out as the coolest thing in the world. In reality people love a smiling face. A smile can relate to anyone, while a frown is only for those who are insecure and probably attempting to prove themselves as someone they are not. So be cool and put a cool, colorful smile on your face.

**Hello, Waving Body Language:** An eyebrow flashing up and down will be seen when this body language comes in contact with someone. The hello body language is one that is ready to say, "Good Morning" or

"Glad to see you." It shares relations with the Open, Friendly Body Language. It is polite and refuses to limit its attention to self, but explores the depth and interest of others. It is the body language that wants to assist in whatever way it can. It is helpful and concerned with what's going on around it. You can always depend on the Hello, Waving Body Language.

**Goofy, Silly Body Language:** Surprisingly, a salesperson who exhibits a goofy, silly body language is likely to make a lot of sales. Why? This body language is seen as non-threatening. You will seem to not be fully aware of your surroundings or what you are doing, but somehow you are capable of getting the job done.

This body language appears to be in a sort of confused, questioning state, not really knowing where it is going but somehow, is still able to get there. Don't be afraid to come across a little silly sometimes.

Many smart people like to use this type of body language to purposely make others underestimate them. And this increases the chance for them to have the advantage in getting what they want out of others. If you are smart, you need not show it all the time. Keep your weaknesses in secrecy, but keep your strengths in greater secrecy until the time is right.

**Humble, Unassuming Body Language:** Humility is more powerful than pride. A humble body language will get you much further and much faster in life than an arrogant one. Pride is for the insecure while humility is for the strong at heart.

A humble body language can get along with anyone because it is very flexible and adaptable to anyone; and not afraid to do anything or appear any way. It will stoop to the floor to get what it wants and is not afraid to get itself a little dirty. With a humble body language, you are not too concerned about how you look; you are more concerned about your purpose to achieve what you are aiming for. This is one of the most powerful body languages to acquire. Do your best to be as humble as you can be, and you will find yourself achieving unprecedented success.

**Innocent, Child-like Body Language:** The body language of innocence makes people say, "Aahhhhh – that's so cute." It makes others want to help you as much as they can. Others will not mind inconveniencing themselves with someone who exhibits an innocent, child-like body language. With this body language your eyes are wide open, trying to comprehend the vastness that's around you. The mouth too, is slightly opened. The arms are swaying freely from side to side. There is little effort in your walk. No real hesitation is observed but only a curiosity to learn more.

**Humorous, Clumsy Body Language:** This body language often does not see where it's going. It often bumps into things. "Be careful," is the thought someone has who observes the humorous, clumsy body language. It doesn't really care how it looks and apparently, it does not care where it's going either, bumping into everything in sight. This body language makes others want to laugh and can be somewhat clown-like. This person's facial expression is a partially blank stare that says, "Huh?"

**Confident, Knowledgeable Body Language:** This body language should be used on those who are looking for a serious, competent person who can do the job right. The shoulders are straight and the chin is level. This body language does not move about or fidget too much because the one with this body language is in control of their thoughts and deliberate movements. With this body language, a determination is in your eye that says, "I am ready to get the job done." This body language is gearing to clasp its hands together and say, "Let's do this."

There is the risk of appearing slightly arrogant with this body language, but there is indeed a difference.

**Enthusiastic, Energetic Body Language:** This body language is hyper, with hands and arms moving all over the place. The face is making one thousand expressions per minute and the person just can't keep still. It's almost as if something is in the pants of the one who possesses this body language. Their facial expression is in the continuous urging state of,

"Come and see what I have here for you." This body language is like a child with a new toy who just can't wait to play.

**Nonchalant, Lacking Effort Body Language:** This body language just really doesn't care if it walks away empty handed. If you want it then here it is; if you don't then, "That's okay with me," are the words expressed by this body language. This can be good in a sense, since most prospects don't like the idea of being pressured. It tells the prospect that you are not desperate and are not in dire need, so it's just a matter of whether they are going to buy "it" or not.

With this body language it is not surprising to see something that appears to be a yawn. Droopy eyes are also expected and the annoying sound of a sigh may be heard. Turning away from the prospect as if it's time to go should not be considered a surprising thing. This body language has a big "whatever" attached to it.

**Non-Judgmental, Simple-Minded Body Language:** This body language does not care who it keeps for company. No company is to be rejected. Any company is good company as is all news good news as far as this body language is concerned. This body language is a co-partner with the Humble, Unassuming Body Language. It does not mind hanging out with the poor and downtrodden; but yet, it somehow manages to keep the company of the rich and famous as well.

This body language does not look at anyone with a snare. The eyes do not penetrate too deeply and the look is always just right. No preconceived notions can be observed and no defensive behavior can be spotted. The arms and legs are as free as a bird's wings. This body language is likely to pat someone on the back as they part from each other. A mutual relationship of good will and ease is established. No discomfort on either side is detected.

**Flirtatious, Sensual Body Language:** This body language is one of seduction. It softly and deeply looks into the eyes of the prospect and finds itself subtly looking down at the nose, and even a slight glance at the lips of the prospect every once in a while. This body language is totally focused on the prospect to an arousing degree. The eyes look deeper and deeper into the prospect's pupil for a little longer than usual. A slight smile often accompanies this look.

The distance between the two people closes in more and more as the conversation continues. A distance of two feet apart is not necessarily considered inappropriate with the one possessing this body language.

A feeling of oneness between the two people can also be observed. A gentle, cozy, good-natured feeling can be felt from across the room. Their breathing is very relaxed and slow.

This body language can feel the aura of the person standing in front of it and wants to exchange aura for aura. Since feelings travel through air, with the utilization of our aura energy, the one possessing the flirtatious body language will imagine their sensual feelings traveling through air, reaching the person who is the target of their sensual admiration.

**Attentive, Caring Body Language:** This is the body language of empathy. It understands what another person is thinking and feels what another person is feeling. It wants to be in the life of the one who is there standing before it.

This body language is not the least bit indifferent to the prospect's concerns. The prospect's concerns are its number one priority. If the prospect hurts then it hurts too. If the prospect is in tears then it will provide a shoulder to cry on. This body language wants to help in the best way possible. It is sincere and true.

This body language wants to understand the prospect's needs. It does so by asking questions and listening caringly. It wants to know what it can do to lend a helping hand. It needs to know what the prospect's likes and dislikes are. Additionally, it wants to align itself with the prospect. It wants to be even more than a salesperson – it wants to be a friend to call upon. It wants to listen and learn. This body language is perhaps the most powerful of all the body languages.

## Body Languages To Avoid:

- ✓ Nervous Body Language
- ✓ Thinking Too Much Body Language
- ✓ Sudden Movement Body Language
- ✓ Impatient Body Language
- ✓ Defensive Body Language
- ✓ Arrogant Body Language
- ✓ Frustrated Body Language
- ✓ Angry Body Language
- ✓ Rigid Body Language
- ✓ Hurried Body Language
- ✓ Uptight Body Language

## How Breathing Rhythm Affects Your Body Language:

If you are upset then your breathing is going to be fast and irregular. Conversely, if you are calm and contented then your breathing is going to be light, slow, deep and even. If you are uncomfortable and uneasy then your breathing will naturally reflect that, but if you can manually take control of your breathing rhythm, then you can alter your body language to match what you want it to be.

In general, you want to be breathing lightly, slowing and evenly to sustain the optimum form of a relaxed body language. If you find yourself uneasy or anxious, make a conscious effort to bring yourself back by manually taking control of your breathing rhythm again. Make an effort to breathe in deeply and slowing, holding it for a few seconds, and exhale with purpose and ease. Repeat this to build back up your composure.

When you find yourself in situations that threaten the stability of your breathing rhythm, remember to manually take back control. Remember, you always want to be breathing slowly, deeply and evenly. This will allow you to sustain a body language of ease, which will in turn put your prospects at ease with you.

❖

To sum it all up, be friendly, relaxed, open, enthusiastic, humble and empathetic, and that should cover the most powerful forms of body language you could ever have.

# Topic 27

## INTERPRETING THE PROSPECT'S BODY LANGUAGE

*A permanent state of transition is man's most noble condition.*
  *- Juan Ramon Jimenez*

All prospects give off cues that indicate how they are feeling unconsciously through their body language. This vital information can be used to change or readjust your presentation to better understand and suite the prospect's needs.

There are ten main aspects you should be looking at when interpreting a prospect's body language and determining how to present your offer:

1. The prospect's pupil size.

2. Whether or not the prospect is folding their arms.

3. Whether or not the prospect has their hands in their pockets.

4. Whether or not the prospect is mirroring and matching your actions.

5. Whether or not the prospect may want some privacy to consider your offer.

6. The prospect's anxiety level.

7. The prospect's level of suspicion.

8. The prospect's comfort level.

9. Whether or not the prospect is responding to your offer in general.

10. The prospect's comfort level towards looking into your eyes.

# 1) The prospect's pupil size:

Many people don't know about the wonder of the pupil. The pupil expands in the dark to bring more light into the eye but the pupil also expands when the individual is experiencing something or someone they like.

You can determine whether or not a prospect is comfortable or even likes you by the size of their pupils. In general, large pupils often indicate a liking for what is being experienced – namely you. Small, tiny, pinhead-sized pupils indicate discomfort or distress. Therefore the larger the prospect's pupils, the more you are being accepted and liked by them.

# 2) Whether or not the prospect is folding their arms:

Unless the prospect is showing other general indications that they are in harmony with you and your message, if their arms are folded then that could be an indication that they are closing their feelings towards you; and that they are uncomfortable or uninterested with the situation.

# 3) Whether or not the prospect has their hands in their pockets:

If a prospect has their hands in their pockets then that could be an indication that they are hiding something, such as their real feelings, or they are exhibiting a superior pose towards you as a salesperson.

# 4) Whether or not the prospect is mirroring and matching your actions:

As noted in an earlier topic, an effective way to influence others is to act like them. If a prospect likes you then they are also going to eventually imitate some of your actions by instinct. Just like husbands and wives naturally imitate each other's acts by instinct, so will/should a prospect imitate some of your natural actions by instinct – which indicates that they are accepting you and your message.

## 5) Whether or not the prospect may want some privacy to consider your offer:

If you feel that the prospect wants to review your offer privately within their own minds secretly or with someone else, the best thing to do is to excuse yourself from the situation and give them time to think. Tell them, "I'll give you some time to think it over." Then walk away. Come back when they show indications that they are ready to proceed. Giving them time to think may double your chances of making a sale.

Don't confuse this subject with Topic 68 – *Don't Give 'Em Time to Think*. There is a subtle difference between the two. Use your discretion if a prospect's body language indicates they need time to absorb your offer; especially if there is someone else with them.

## 6) The prospect's anxiety level:

If a prospect seems to be concerned with time or distracted in general, for example, by looking at their watch, ask them how much time do they have available. A prospect will not absorb your message if their mind is somewhere else because of the simple fact that they may need to be someplace else at a certain time. If you detect this anxiety then tailor your presentation to accommodate the situation. You may have to re-schedule.

## 7) The prospect's level of suspicion:

A prospect usually will not buy anything from a salesperson they don't trust. If you detect any suspicion from them towards you as a salesperson then change your pitch by being upfront with them the best way you can, or else you will lose the sale. Confess to them something that they may want to hear, like a flaw that exists within your product. Show them your weak side but then be sure to provide a reasonable explanation afterwards.

## 8) The prospect's comfort level:

If a prospect seems uncomfortable during your presentation then ask them straight out, "Is there something you are not comfortable with?"

According to their response, change or tailor your presentation to bring them back to a comfort level that both of you can feed off of.

## 9) Whether or not the prospect is responding to your offer in general:

If the prospect is not responding to you then that could be an indication that they may not be interested in your offer at all or that they are not listening to you for the simple fact that you did not do a good job in building rapport. If it's the latter reason then stop your presentation and re-institute a relationship by getting the prospect on your side. Compliment them, find some common ground, use your sense of humor – do whatever it takes to get them to like, trust and bond with you.

## 10) The prospect's comfort level towards looking into your eyes:

It's going to be hard selling to prospects who have a difficult time looking into your eyes. If they are uncomfortable doing such a basic act then it means that the bond between the two of you does not exist. You may want to scrap your whole presentation and go back to the drawing board – try some chitchat to develop a quick friendship with that prospect. In other words, you will need to stop selling the product or service and start selling yourself in order to gain, or regain, the prospect's trust.

❖

As a salesperson it is essential for you to observe the body language cues your prospect may be sending off. Change and adapt are your key words to dealing with a prospect whose body language is not in touch with your message.

# Topic 28

---

## THE UNIVERSAL PERSONALITY CODE

*I present myself to you in a form suitable to the relationship I wish to achieve with you.*
  *- Luigi Pirandello*

*I am a part of all that I have met.*
  *- Lord Tennyson Alfred*

The universal personality code is a personality that can get along with anybody. With this code you do not mold into the prospect's personality but rather, you allow them to mold into your personality. It is the personality of synergy.

There are many different types of personalities and even different astrological signs associated with these personalities. With the universal personality code, you bypass all of this. You defy gravity by lifting yourself above all the rules and regulations and barriers that keep us from getting to know each other.

With the universal personality code you don't care what type of personality the prospect has because you are going to mold them to fit your personality, anyway. A little of you is going to rub off on them a lot. With the universal personality code your aim is to make others into your own image; to make them act how you act and think how you think. Your aim is to transform their natural behavior to be compatible with yours. This may sound like a challenging thing to do but it might be easier than you think.

With the universal personality code you lead by example. You do not allow the other person's action or behavior to affect your performance. You do not allow their personality type to draw you closer or push you away. You do not give in to their negative personality, but you adapt to it,

114

with the knowledge that you will get through to them with your own personality code.

The two main prerequisites you will need to transform anyone to fit into your own personality are: 1) To be willing to communicate with them in the first place and 2) To accept them for who they are.

## Be Willing To Communicate With Them

Your first step to communicating and relating to anyone starts with your *willingness* to communicate with them. Once you learn to overcome that *avoidance code*, then you are 80 percent closer to achieving your goal of communicating with anyone. The main reason why people find it hard to relate with others is merely because they are afraid to approach and learn from the other person. Get over your intimidation of others and you will see how eager they will be towards letting you in, to let you know who they really are. *Intimidation* is the main word that prevents us from getting to know each other. Intimidation creates ignorance and a stagnation that prevents us from knowing and really learning from each other. You will find that once you lose your avoidance code we are all very much alike deep down inside. Everybody will become a nice person once we let go of our intimidation towards them. If we show intimidation then others will put up their usual wall, thereby making it more intimidating for us to get to know them.

## Accept Them For Who They Are

Everybody wants to be accepted for who they are. People are who they are and the way they are because they don't know how to be any other way. You are not an appointed federal judge on how people should act, are you? Therefore, do not believe that you have the right to judge others or act in any self-righteous way that hinders you from really getting to know them. Anyone who detects that you're willing to accept them – with all their faults, flaws, and arrogance – will allow you to really get to know them for who they are. And who they are is something totally different from what you see on the outside. On the inside we are all *softies*. If you don't accept everyone for who they are, then they will put up the  Berlin Wall again, and really make it difficult for you, again. Make it easy on yourself by making an effort to accept others for who they are, and they will make it easy for you. Remember, if you accept others for who they are – no matter how *bad* or obnoxious they may seem – then they will reveal to you that they aren't so bad after all.

❖

Do you realize how successful you will be by applying the universal personality code with your prospects? If you can bypass all the barriers that prevent us from truly getting to know and feel comfortable with each other, then you have opened up the gateway to paradise here on earth. Once a prospect realizes you are not uncomfortable about being around them then you have achieved 80 percent of your goal of making the sale.

# Topic 29

## FIND YOUR PROSPECT'S HOT BUTTONS

*Remember that what pulls the strings is the force hidden within; there lies the power to persuade, there the life – there, if one must speak out, the real man.*
  *-Marcus Aurelius Antoninus*

Hot buttons are topics that excite the prospect. You can find a prospect's hot buttons by asking them questions. The most specific question to ask them is to find out what they like. From their response you will tailor your presentation to focus on what turns them on.

Sometimes a prospect will not tell you or let you know what their hot buttons are because they may want to keep it secret. In this case you may have to coax it out of them or simply throw out issues that you think may be of great interest to them. You will know your prospect's hot buttons by appealing to their emotions and their senses.

You only need to ask the prospect one particular question which comes in many forms, to discover what their hot buttons are. This question unlocks the secret code that uncovers what will excite that prospect. The question in its basic form would follow either of these patterns:

> **"What do you like *most* about X?"**
> **"What are you looking for *most* in X?"**
> **"What is *most* important to you about X?"**

Examples are:
✓ *What do you like most about* your current service?"
✓ *What do you like most about* the product you're looking for?"
✓ *What do you like most about* the car you want to look at?"
✓ *What do you like most about* fishing?

117

This question asks specifically what the prospect is looking for. It narrows everything down into perspective and gives the reason that motivates the prospect to part with their money. It also answers the question of what motivated the prospect to even consider their purchase. This question alone – if answered honestly by the prospect – will give you most of the ammunition needed to put your presentation in a way that will satisfy the prospect's needs or wants.

**After the prospect answers your question of what they like most, or what they are looking for most, then follow up by asking them: "Why is that so important to you?" or "Why do you like that so much?"**

Once the prospect gives you the true answer of "why" they like what they like, then you can tailor the sale to emphasize that you have everything they like. You will be able to zoom into your presentation specifically on only those things they like, that you can offer them. But it doesn't stop there.

Once the prospect gives you the answer to what they like most about X, your job is to ask them a very important follow up question. And that second question is:

**"What else do you like most about X?"**

The prospect may respond by giving additional reasons why they like the product or service, or they may only be focused on their one original reason. If they give additional reasons then tap into them and tailor your presentation even more by focusing on those other things that makes the prospect like the product or service.

Once the prospect tells you what they like then half the battle is won. A prospect who tells you what they like and what makes them like what they like is Samson telling Delilah the secret to his strength. Once you discover what makes the prospect strong, then you are able the focus your presentation by revealing and demonstrating to them that you have what they want. This is accomplished by showing them the features and by demonstrating the benefits in accordance with how it will fit into that prospect's life.

If the prospect doesn't tell you the answer of what they like, you can read between the lines by what they say, with the words they choose. Look for words with an emotional theme to them such as, "We like the smell of the roses" – the sense of smell being the emotional stimuli here. Some prospects will make life easier for you by saying what their likes are without having to ask. This is why it is always a good idea to be in the listening mode.

Once you've discovered what a prospect likes and why they like it, don't let go of that valuable information; for that information is the hot button that will make them buy from you. Eat up this information as if it was you're favorite meal of the day. Encourage your mind to remember each and every benefit your service or product carries that specifically fit the requirements of what the prospect likes.

Sometimes your product or service may not contain the hot button(s) the prospect is looking for; but if it does, then keep on pressing that button from red to green, until the whole room is lit up.

# Topic 30

---

## USE THE SENSE OF HUMOR TO LIGHTEN UP THE MOOD: IT'S EASY

*Laughter is the shortest distance between two people.*
        *- Victor Borge*

The sense of humor will always lighten up an intense situation, like the color blue can put you in a good mood. The sense of humor should have been called the sense of healing because that is what it does. Humor heals everything.

Humor is not memorizing, using or laughing at jokes. Humor is really the idea of taking life and its challenges lightly. For example, if you find yourself constantly running into challenging situations that are threatening to wear you down, you could fall under the pressure and let it keep you down, or you could rise up to the challenge and face it head on. If you decide to do the latter then you have most likely discovered humor.

Humor is unloading the heavy loads of life with your wit and charm. Humor is taking everything that is a problem with a grain of salt. Humor is a brick in one hand and a feather in the other, weighing the balance of life.

If you choose the path of weighing the balance of life with the feather, then you have discovered the pathway to humor. Humor is the ability to lighten all situations that are heavy. Humor is to put all your burdens down and rest against walls of Jell-O.

Once you discover what humor is, then you will be more likely to use it. The byproduct of humor is what we know as *telling jokes*. Once you understand that anything can be weighed like a feather in your hand, then you are bound to tickle others with your jokes. Once you understand that everything has a silly side to it, then you will be prone to laugh at yourself and all your mishaps. This truly is the sense of humor in motion.

Humor is not telling jokes – humor is the tickle you get from that feather in the palm of your hand. Life is definitely not as gloomy as we sometimes make it out to be, and since we only live once, that should inspire us to live our lives to the fullest. Let us make the most out of it by enjoying the best of it.

In sales, humor is finding a way to give your prospect the feather you carry in the palm of your hand. With selling, humor is seeking a method to tickle the prospect with that feature you see rubbing up against their nose. "Hachew!" Bless you. In sales, humor is transferring your ticklish feeling with the ticklish feeling that we all carry.

Don't be afraid to use humor as much as you can in all your sale endeavors.

Prospects and customers like humor even though they may hide the fact. Even though some of them will not want to admit they like it, always approach each sale endeavor with a degree of humor. Don't be hesitant or shy to point out the silly side of life, which tickles your funny bone. If it's funny to you, it's most likely funny to your prospect, unless you're being a "weirdo" in other ways not specified. Keep your jokes clean with your prospects and you'll do fine.

You will have an advantage above other salespeople if you decide to add humor to your sales presentations. Try it and you'll see. Practice this technique to yourself if need be. As long as it's clean and appropriate, and as long as you like it, your prospects too will like it. And then you will have scored yourself another 50 points. If your presentation needs to be professional, then consider having it 90% professional and 10% humorous. If your prospect is easy to get along with, then consider being 50% professional and 50% humorous. And if your prospect is really cool, then consider being 100% humorous in your presentation, unless otherwise specified.

# Topic 31

---

## BELIEF IN YOURSELF IS THE KEY
## TOWARDS ACHIEVING ALL GOALS! - Part I

*The best bet is to bet on yourself.*
*- Arnold Glasow*

There is something that is familiar with almost all successful people – they like to brag about themselves, to themselves! They like to use phrases such as:

> **"I'm the best."**
> **"I'm good at what I do."**
> **"Not too many people can beat me."**
> **"Check me out."**
> **"I always win."**
> **"I'm good at it."**
> **"I still got it!"**
> **"Sometimes, I just amaze myself."**
> **"I can sell to a wooden statue."**
> **"I'm so great."**

You may have heard or known that successful people think this way; but even if you've never heard them say such things, believe it – they do indeed think such things.

Why do they say such things to themselves? Answer: to boost their ego and to remind themselves never to forget themselves. This is called *self-belief*!

Sometimes, insecure people will say those same, exact phrases too, but the difference is, the ones who are genuine believe in what they are thinking.

You must start bragging about yourself and mean it, if you plan to start seriously believing in yourself. What have you got to lose? Nothing! On the contrary, there is much to gain.

*Belief in yourself* is the key that will open all doors that lead to success. Start, therefore, to believe in yourself from today onwards. Remember, you can accomplish anything you put your mind to. Your wish is your command.

Keep on boasting about yourself, to yourself. Every time you do something desirable or that was successful, pat yourself on the back and exaggerate, if need be, about your fine talent.

Whatever you desire, say that you are it, even if you have not accomplished it yet. Believe that you will accomplish it because it's only a matter of time; and then you shall have it!

"How can I start to believe in myself?" you may ask. You do so by recognizing and listening to the voices in your head. How can you tell that you are disbelieving in yourself? You can by recognizing and listening to the voices in your head. If they are saying mostly negative things such as "You can't…" then you must change those *can'ts* into *can*. Say, "I can. I can. I can. I know I can. I will. I will. I will! I am. I am. I am!" And so it shall be done.

How do you believe in something that you don't believe in, but want to believe? You do so by silencing the negative voices, then by introducing new positive voices. Repetition is the key here. Keep on telling yourself you can do it. Consider the positive voices more genuine than the negative ones.

When you feel that useless feeling coming upon you when you are striving towards believing in yourself, *ignore* it. Keep on going about your business. Eventually those, "I can't do it," feelings will retreat. You are already the victor – you only need to realize and accept it.

For this is the key to believing in yourself – to think and act as if you've already achieved what you desire to have or become. Then you shall have it. Your wish is your command! Anything you desire – just believe that it's yours already, and you shall have it.

# Topic 32

## BELIEF IN YOURSELF IS THE KEY TOWARDS ACHIEVING ALL GOALS! - Part II

*A man's doubts and fears are his worst enemies.*
  *- William Wrigley, Jr.*

In the most extreme case of its definition, to believe in yourself means that you think you're better than most people when it comes to your ability to do your job. In its most blunt definition, self-belief means you have a secret ego that tells you that you are on top, above all the little people below. In the most graphic terminology, belief in one's self means that you are not in the crowd, but over the crowd. While it does not mean that you think you are better than others, it does mean that you think you're better than others in your abilities.

Doubt is the *only* force that stands in your way towards believing in yourself. Only if you learn how to suppress doubt will you be successful in believing in yourself. Doubt is the enemy of self-belief. It is the thorn in self-belief's flesh. If you can pull doubt out of you then you will be free to accomplish your goals. A new relief will come upon you, and your belief will set you free.

Once you discover how to remove doubt from every fiber of your being then you will develop wings that will make you fly. You will soar above and beneath the clouds with your new sense of freedom to explore. But with doubt, your wings are replaced with stubs, and your sense to explore replaced with darkness and gloom.

Belief in yourself only need be a little stronger than your doubt; and that belief will take care of your doubt. Doubt cannot win with a belief system that is even a grain of salt larger. Your belief system will quickly multiply the day that it gains one iota of advantage over your doubt.

Doubt and belief cannot co-exist comfortably with each other. The house of self-belief is not big enough to accommodate a guest such as doubt. Doubt must leave immediately.

This is the way you must look at it: Doubt is competing to occupy your mind over your belief system, and you must accept the challenge. You must not shy away from the competition or else doubt will always serve as an intimidation factor, like a bulldog stationed at a warehouse.

You must arm yourself with the necessary tools and ammunition to rid doubt from the gateway of your freedom and success. And the only way to do this is to face doubt head on.

Do not be afraid of doubt, which pretends and portrays itself to be a tough-guy – a bully who likes to boss everyone around. But in reality, doubt is a pussycat when put to the challenge. Like a bulldog that barks but has no bite, is the real doubt!

You may have been allowing doubt to take a hold of you for the longest while, maybe even all your life, and you probably didn't even know you had a tenant named doubt in your house. But now you know, and you know what you have to do. Arm yourself and be ready for battle. How dare doubt corrupt the pathway to success that is rightfully yours! Will you allow doubt to occupy what is deservingly yours? Is not Doubt a thief? He pays no rent and has been living in the mansion that is your inheritance from birth. But it's time for doubt to pay up and pay big. Yes! Doubt will pay you every penny he owes, and that is where your self-belief comes in.

You will no longer be a victim of the threats and vandalism from the imposter named doubt. You will no longer be a silent witness while this bastard named doubt eats your food and drinks your wine. You will no longer be a spectator while doubt sleeps in your bed and pisses in your toilet. It's time for you to take charge. You are the landlord of your own house now. Kick doubt out like the dog he is. You own this house.

# Topic 33

## BELIEF IN YOURSELF IS THE KEY TOWARDS ACHIEVING ALL GOALS! - Part III

*Perhaps I am stronger than I think.*
  *- Thomas Merton*

Belief in yourself is all you need to do whatever you put your mind to, just like it is wings are all a bird needs to fly. Once you have that gut belief in yourself then there is nothing you cannot do. This is the only tool that is multi-purpose in doing all tasks. Belief in yourself will make you the master of your world. Belief in yourself means you are the King or Queen Midas where everything you touch turns into gold. Ask any successful person how they became successful, and they will most likely refer you to their self-belief. Why do some people succeed over others? It is by the measure of their self-belief. The stronger you believe in yourself, the more you will succeed over other people, and the more you will accomplish in this life. Belief in one's self is what makes most, if not all, successful people who they are.

  Belief in yourself will tell you all things. Don't worry about what you don't know – your self-belief will whisper instructions to your ears. You will eventually have full command over whatever you don't know once you're equipped with self-belief. Your belief will make sure you know. Don't worry about anything – belief in yourself will watch your back and take good care of you. All your doubts and insecurities will disintegrate if even you carry just a trace of self-belief. Of all things, self-belief is the one thing you must have to conquer all other things. With this tool you will be the master builder of all projects.

## What Does It Mean To Believe In Yourself?:

To believe in yourself is to simply know that you can successfully accomplish what you want done. In sales, belief in yourself means that you are good at changing minds through persuasive maneuvering. It's not a matter of if you will get it done, but of how soon. You already see it done in your mind, now all you have to do is follow through with your actions.

## The Feeling That Comes From Believing In Yourself:

You will experience a distinct feeling in your gut that will let you know if self-belief is within you. As belief in yourself grows, you will develop a gut feeling that tells you, "Yes. I'm feeling it. I know it's there. I can do this." If your stomach feels empty, devoid or hollow, then you'll know that you still have some "impregnation" to do. The belief that you can accomplish your endeavor will fill your stomach pretty much the same way liquid does. Belief will make you feel full of energy, determination and surety. This is one of the physical signs that belief is present within you.

## The Second Image Of Yourself:

Belief in yourself means that every time you stand before a prospect, you are also standing behind them. What does that mean? In other words, your presence and ability are so strong that it's almost as if there are two of you – that you have your own self as a back up, like a mirror image of yourself to fill the gaps and to help wherever you are lacking. So even with your shortcomings, there is always someone – specifically your other self – to pull you back up. Your presence will be so strong that it is almost as if there are two of you. Therefore, when interacting with prospects, remember to imagine yourself surrounding them with your presence and overcoming them with your strong belief and conviction in what you have to offer them.

## You Are In Control Of The Situation

You will always be in control of any situation if you are in control of yourself; and the only way to be in control of yourself is to know yourself. And to know yourself is to believe in yourself. Once you understand that you can control any situation inasmuch as you are able to control your self-belief, then success will be yours. If you believe in yourself then your prospects will believe in you too.

There is a certain aura that someone who believes in themselves carries; and that aura is felt by prospects who interact with you. An aura that says *everything is going well* will also convince your prospects that everything is indeed well. All you need to do is simply believe that you're in control of your world because no one can control your world for you. And once you realize and practice this belief, then you are indeed in control of your world. When you are in control of your world then others will naturally lean towards you because they want to learn what it is that makes up you and your world.

# Topic 34

---

## MENTALLY COMMAND IT, AND IT SHALL HAPPEN AS YOU WILL

*You give birth to that on which you fix your mind.*
*- Antoine de Saint-Exupery*

*A person under the firm persuasion that he can command resources virtually has them.*
*- Titus Livy*

There are many hidden secrets that we do not yet understand, much less know about. One of these secrets is a phenomenon in which what one thinks and commands in their own mind – without using words – can actually make another person do it; no matter the distance between both people. They could even be thousands of miles apart. The key is to make the command clear, short and direct, using four words or less.

Examples:

| | |
|---|---|
| **Call Me** | **Come Here** |
| **Buy It Now** | **Come To Me** |
| **Love Me** | **Believe Me** |
| **Stay With Me** | **Take It** |
| **Trust Me** | **Say Yes** |
| **Wait!** | **Listen To Me** |
| **Give Me Your Number** | **Look At Me** |
| **Get Excited** | **Feel Good** |
| **Come See Me** | **Call Mom** |
| **Get Excited** | |

I heard about this phenomenon quite some time ago but had not taken it seriously. Then one day I realized that my prospects were not responding to the door tags I was leaving at their homes. I recalled this remote mind-to-mind telepathic form of communication and used it. In my mind I said, "Call me," and aimed it at all those potential clients. That was it.

Within half an hour I received a call from one of those prospects who requested my services as quickly as possible. Then within another half an hour, I received a call from a girlfriend who had not called me in many days. Another hour later I received another call from that first prospect who had called me earlier, to let me know that they really wanted me to come as soon as possible. From then on, I did not need any more convincing that this technique really works.

From that point onwards, anything I wished a person to do, I simply commanded in my mind that they should do it. Of course I do not receive success 100% of the time – probably not even 25% of the time, but I receive enough success to realize that I'm much better off using this method than not using it.

Whatever you desire a person to do, just command it and so it will be. Believing that it will happen increases your chances of it actually happening. In fact, the more you believe, the more it will happen. Thinking as though that person was right in front of you will make your task seem easier to accomplish.

What you think can be more powerful than what you say, in terms of making a person heed to your wishes. Your mind will connect to that person's subconscious more readily since you are using a mind-to-mind connection. By using this technique the prospect will feel as if they are acting of their own will, as opposed to you allowing them to think and act a certain way. Try this method and see what happens. Your wish is their bidding! Wish it and they shall obey. Think it and it shall happen – not always, but sometimes is better than none.

## How to use this technique:

One way of using this technique is to imagine yourself in a quiet place, like a bedroom with closed doors; with no noise coming in or going out. Now imagine yourself peacefully commanding what you wish. Think it to yourself naturally and imagine the recipient receiving your message. Don't force it, but be firm and direct. Focus on the recipient; imagine the person is hearing and receiving your command. Believe they have heard your wish. Do this, and they will, even without them knowing it. They will think it was their own thought.

## How it works:

If it was something the recipient might have naturally considered – even to a small degree – then they will feel compelled to act upon it. You cannot force them to do something they don't want to do – but you can encourage them to do something they might have already considered doing. If the recipient does not respond then maybe your belief was not strong enough, or then again maybe the recipient is just not in the least bit interested!

**Note**: Use this and any other method like it for a good cause and not for a devious or malicious cause because the bad we do and wish comes back to us eventually. For instance, don't wish to sleep with another man's wife, or else you may find yourself in the same situation of being constantly cheated on.

# Topic 35

---

## IT'S NOT A MATTER OF IF YOU WILL, BUT OF HOW SOON YOU WILL

*I think, therefore I am.*
*- René Descartes*

If you believe you are good at selling then it will not be a matter of *if* you will sell, but of *how soon* you will. Timing, as in how quickly, will be the factor that motivates your ego. How quickly you can "get it done" will be the talk of the town, rather than, "Let's hope you get it done."

Learn to program your mind from thinking in the *if* mode to the *how soon* mode. This takes strong, real belief in yourself that you can do it. This way of thinking will also increase your belief in yourself, especially if you are seeing results right before your eyes. Bypass the word "suppose" or the phrase "let's see what happens," and all the many variations, and turn them into "let's see how soon I can make it happen." This form of thinking will speed up your success and sale numbers dramatically. Why? Simply because you're changing from the *if* mode to the *how soon* mode. This can be accomplished because you know that it will happen. The question is not if you will make it happen, but how good and quick you are at making it happen.

With this mentality it's not a matter of if you will pass your math test, but of how high your grade will be. It's not a matter of if you will find the woman or man of your dreams, but of how soon you will. It's not a matter of if you will be successful this year, but of how successful and how quickly that success will arrive. It's not a matter of if you will overcome any obstacles or shortcomings in your way, but of how soon you will pass through these challenges. With this method of thinking it's not a matter of *if* you can do it, but of *how soon* you can do it. The

132

bottom line is: you already know you can do it, and now it's just a matter of time.

## The *how soon* mode:

If you want to be successful in life, think in the *how soon* mode. If you want to be unsure and insecure about your success then think in the *if* mode. *How soon* is the phrase that runs through the mind of every successful person and every successful thought. *How soon* is very popular and common with those who know what the word "achievement" means. *How soon* gets straight to the point, like an arrow hits the bull's-eye and scores. *How soon* are the guiding words to all those who want to know success. First came the chicken, then came the egg. First came the *how soon*, then came the *how to*.

It is recorded in the Scriptures that a certain disciple with others in a boat found themselves in a storm at sea. This disciple then saw Jesus. Jesus allowed him to step out of the boat to walk on the water to come towards Him. Jesus wanted this certain disciple to keep his focus on Him so he would not sink. This disciple stepped out of the boat and attempted to do as Jesus had instructed; but whenever he saw the waters raging and took his focus off Jesus, he found himself beginning to sink. But when he refocused his attention, and with the help of Jesus, he remained afloat. In the same manner, if you want to be successful, you need to be bold and focus on the words *how soon*. Bypass the words *how to* and just focus on *how soon*, and the *how to* will come immediately afterwards. If you want to sink then focus on the word *if*.

It's not a matter of if you will sell, but of *how soon* you will. Time yourself. When you decide that this will be your method of thinking when it comes to selling, the *how to* will naturally be easier to accomplish. Why? It's only a matter of time.

Therefore envision a timeline whereby you are going to make success happen before thinking about the *how to* of making that success happen. It's not a matter of if you will sell, it's not even a matter of when you will sell – but of *how soon* you will. Why? Simply because you know you will.

# Topic 36

---

## BELIEVE IN THE IMPOSSIBLE THOUGHTS

*Only those who dare to fail greatly can ever achieve greatly.*
  *- Robert F. Kennedy*

*We aim above the mark to hit the mark.*
  *- Ralph Waldo Emerson*

What would you say if you were asked, "Do you believe you can fly?" If your answer was "No," then you would be right. If your answer was "Yes," then you would be crazy, for not even I believe that you can fly. I can't fly either but the bottom line is this – if you believe you can't do something then you're right. It is very unlikely that you will accomplish what you don't believe you can successfully achieve. Your ability is only limited by your belief in yourself.

Do you believe that you can gain two million dollars in two years? If you say "No," then you are right. You will probably not gain two million dollars in the next two years, primarily because you don't believe you can. Regardless of your current financial circumstances, if someone asks you if you believe that you'll gain two million dollars in two years, then your answer should be "Yes!" Your degree of success will depend upon how much you believe in that thought.

You must believe in the impossible thoughts if you want to achieve your impossible dreams. Believe in the impossible and you will achieve it. Nothing is impossible.

You are only limited in your ability inasmuch as you are limited in your thoughts. If you don't believe you will ever make a million dollars a year then you never will. The reason is because those self-made millionaires who make a million dollars each year actually hope to make ten million dollars each year. Indeed, they have greater dreams and thoughts than what they are currently accomplishing. If they had desired to make a

134

million dollars each year then they may have only been making one hundred thousand dollars instead. If they were actually making ten million dollars each year then it means that their goal was to make one hundred million each year.

People who dream great big fantastic dreams never reach them because their dreams are continually expanding as they get closer and closer towards achieving their goals. Dreamers never really want to reach their goals – their hope is to expand their goals as soon as their original goal is close at hand. They dream impossible dreams and imagine great thoughts because enough is never enough for the man or woman with ambition. Ambition is imagining yourself ten times greater than who or what you currently are. And when you've achieved that greatness then it creates another ambition, greater than the one before it. A man with great ambition can never achieve it because he loves dreaming incredible dreams.

In sales, if you want to achieve great success then have impossible thoughts and dream great dreams. Don't be complacent or satisfied with what you have or else you will lose momentum; and whatever you currently have will wither away. Keep up with your imagination, renew your dreams, update your thoughts and wonder of bigger and greater things, and success shall be yours.

If you want to succeed in sales then don't try to reach your numbers. Instead, try to exceed your numbers. Have no limits to your numbers. May your limitations be as vast as the ocean. Open the gateway to wealth and abundance by never putting a latch on it. Exceed your quota, dream greater dreams, wish of mightier goals and the world shall be yours.

Believe that you can do better than the best competitors in the business. Don't consider them as the untouchable or the unreachable. Instead consider them the best, but only for now. There is someone else who's coming along. And her hair blows in the wind. And her clothing is made of fine linen. And there shall be no end to her reign.

So think thoughts that will make others laugh at you. Dream dreams that will make others giggle behind your back. Say things to yourself that will make you wonder about your own sanity. Believe in things that you do not believe in. Entertain your most impossible thoughts. Begin doing this right now!

# Topic 37

## PERSISTENCY IS THE FORCE THAT KEEPS THE BALL ROLLING!

*A winner never quits and a quitter never wins.*
  *- Anonymous*

*Don't leave before the miracle happens.*
  *- Anonymous*

*Effort is only effort when it begins to hurt.*
  *- Jose' Ortega Y Gasset*

Persistency does not take "no" for an answer the first or second time around; it only hears the word "no" when it is said the third time, and even then it shrugs it off as if it was the first. Persistency will need to hear "no" at least two more times before coming to the conclusion that it must start all over again, either later on or another day. Thus the law of persistency is that it does not hear the first two "no's," and only begins to heed after hearing it three more times.

Persistency is deaf to rejections and ignorant to excuses and objections. Persistency does not understand things very well unless it is those very things that it is seeking to hear. Any other sound to its ears is gibberish.

Though persistency may be hard of hearing, it is not lacking when it comes to producing results. Persistency is the partner of any salesperson who seriously intends to be successful in the Sales business.

Persistency is the refusal to give up on anything easily. Persistency is the knowledge that every prospect is not going to be interested until you twist their arm a little bit. Persistency is the next step with that same prospect before stepping on to a next prospect. Persistency is the hands of a clock ticking for another 60 seconds. Persistency is the stubbornness not to give up. Persistency is the sentence that does not have a full stop. Persistency is the daughter of determination.

Studies done in the latter half of the twentieth century have shown that most prospects will not buy anything from a salesperson unless that salesperson asks for the sale at least four times. The problem is that most salespeople give up after the first, second or third objection. If they had only persisted one more time, then more often than not they would have made the sale.

Persistency is the force that keeps the ball rolling. If you give up easily in an effort to make a sale, then your ball will stay buried in a ditch. You must experiment and find multiple ways to keep a conversation going so that you can ask for the sale again and again. For it is a conversation that is the raw material needed to ask for something over and over again. Without the structure of a conversation, all you'll have is a mechanical repetitious phrase without meaning.

Try striking up and holding a conversation with your prospect. The more you hold on to the conversation, the more you will be able to inject reasons why the prospect should buy your product, over and over again. If they object then you'll ask them why?

Keep the conversation going by asking questions and learning what makes the prospect like what they like or dislike what they dislike. Consider yourself as a problem solver who can greatly assist the prospect gain their needs and wants.

Don't give up after the first, second or third excuse a prospect gives you and you'll be fine. Excuses are just the prospect's insecurities coming forward. They don't know any better and use words to create a barrier. Prospects hate uncertainty and change, and it's up to you to reassure them that they are in safe hands by specifically pointing out what they are about to gain, and not lose, by taking your advice. Remember, as a salesperson you are there to serve and provide the best or most convenient service to your prospects. Don't let them push you away with the first, second or third "no." Sometimes "no" means "yes" if you stick around just a little while longer.

If you can endure a barrage of "no's" from a prospect and still find the willpower to keep on going, the prospect will admire you for your tenacity. They'll want to know what fuels your determination. They will long to learn what keeps your fire burning. "Doesn't water put out this fire of yours?" Don't let their floods of rain put out your flames. Sometimes prospects say "no" with the intent to say "yes," if you can endure the plight.

# Topic 38

## DETERMINATION IS WHAT CAUSES DESIRABLE END RESULTS!

*Fall seven times, stand up eight.*
*- Japanese proverb*

Determination is a wonderful word and even more so, an incredible deed. If you apply determination to anything you do, you stand a greater chance to succeed. Determination will find a way when there is no way. Determination makes the impossible possible. With determination, failure is never an option. Why?

**Determination completes everything.**
**Everything is born of determination.**

✓ Determination is that which makes the world go round.
✓ Determination is the first and the last – the beginning, the end!
✓ Determination is the sun that rises in the morning breeze.
✓ A house that was built on solid rock is determination.
✓ It was the poor man who became rich that symbolizes determination.
✓ For determination is that mental muscle which will fight against the odds, and still be crowned victorious in the end.

If you keep determination by your side – as you stride towards completing your tasks – then you have chosen a worthy companion. Determination is stronger than you, and will strengthen all your weaknesses. He will make you firm where you are feeble. He will fill up the gap in those qualities you are lacking. He will do whatever it takes to make you a success. Determination will push you forward. He will not allow you to give up. He will pick you up when you fall and mend your broken heart. He will fit together again that which was shattered. Determination is the inventor of all things beautiful – a wonderful thing indeed. With determination you are bound to succeed at almost anything you put your mind to. Once you start with determination by your side, there is no turning back. Determination does not know what's behind him because he only pushes forward. Wisdom will let you know what's behind.

Determination does not know how to quit; instead he just keeps on going, and going, and going, and going, and going until he gets what he wants. He's been known to get himself into trouble sometimes, for he is a stubborn bastard. But the good news is this: the reward that he produces is well worth the effort.

There is no politically correct way to put this, but determination is simply an idiot because he does not know when to stop. He does not know what the word "no" or the suggestion *quit* means. He does not know what the phrase "Give it a break" means either.

Though determination may lack certain words in his vocabulary, he will still be the master of his domain because he knows what the word "success" means. Determination is a confident man ready to claim his bride.

Persistency is the daughter of determination. Both work hand in hand to take what they know is theirs. Beware – this is not a dysfunctional family. Determination taught persistency everything she knows.

Determination is picturing the future the way you want it to be, and then turning your world into that picture that it should be. Determination is what makes you get up each morning to accomplish what you have to do. Determination is a life brought into this world. In sales, determination is doing whatever you NEED to do, so that you can accomplish whatever else you need to do.

Please don't confuse determination with desperation – desperation is almost the opposite of determination. Desperation is despair, while determination is purpose. Determination is what causes desirable end results!

# Topic 39

## FOCUS ON YOUR PURPOSE AND FEEL THE PLEASURE

*Keep your eyes on the stars but keep your feet on the ground.*
  *- Theodore Roosevelt*

*The purpose of life is a life of purpose.*
  *- Robert Byrne*

If you were traveling on a long ride to the beach, then your focus on the road would be necessary to produce the desired results. During sexual intercourse your focus must be on the issue at hand to produce the desired results. To get an A+ in math your focus on logic and the details of numbers must be pursued to get the desired results. Similarly, in sales, if you want to sell, sell, SELL, then your focus must be on the method of selling to produce the desire results.

Focus creates a pleasurable feeling because it produces desired results. That is why successful people who focus on the task at hand usually enjoy their work because it produces a type of euphoria, a type of pleasure, knowing that results will happen. The person who gets an A+ on their math test may be the most aroused person in the classroom because their focus produced pleasure and satisfaction.

Focusing puts you into a type of trance. There is indeed a great feeling of arousal when you focus on something. It forces you to put all your energy, thoughts and feelings to the issue at hand; and that is what makes it so exciting. It brings you into another world – a world you can enjoy being in; a world of peace, bliss and quietness; a world you can call you own.

When you focus on your purpose you will find yourself in your own Garden of Eden – a place where you can relax and enjoy, and have fun; a world you may find hard to leave because it's so pleasurable.

Whatever your purpose is, focus on it, and you will find yourself loving it. You will find yourself wanting to be indulged with that purpose. You will find yourself being enraptured by that purpose. That is why you'll find some people enjoy doing certain things hour after hour, day after day; because they have become enraptured by their focus.

Pay attention to what you need to accomplish, and you will find success all around you. Don't worry about success because success will take care of you if you take care of what you need to do. Success focuses on those who focus on what they should be focusing on.

Why do you think business people like to play golf? Is it because they get to hit a golf ball into a hole? No! The main reason is because it helps them to focus. It helps them to create new ideas for their business and to relax and feel the pleasure of focusing. Whether it be golf or any other sport or activity, they do it because of the pleasurable feeling they get by focusing, which creates pleasure, satisfaction and a sense of achievement.

If you want to feel the sense of pleasure, satisfaction and achievement, then focus on your purpose. Focus on completing your task. Focus on doing a good job. Focus on achieving your goal. Focus, and you will feel how pleasant it is to be an achiever. Focus on the words on this page. See yourself achieving your goals even before you achieve them. Focus on becoming a winner. Focus on what you're going to do with all that cash, relationships and joy that your efforts will produce. Focus on being your own boss. Focus on being able to purchase the material things you want and need. Focus on being thankful for what you already have; because what you already have – no matter how little or great it is – will be the foundation to produce greater things. You are the fruit tree; your focusing will produce fruit year after year if you don't lose a grip on that focus. But why should you lose a grip of your focus? Who wants to let go of the pleasure of being able to have the freedom to enjoy what they've achieved?

There is a pleasure in focusing on selling. Selling is persuading others to buy from you. When others buy from you, it makes you feel good, and gives you the proud sense of satisfaction. And when you're satisfied, you like what you do. Focus on selling and feel the pleasure.

# Topic 40

---

## THREE DEEDS THAT WILL GUARANTEE YOUR SUCCESS AS A SALESPERSON

*Always aim for achievement, and forget about success.*
          *- Helen Hayes*

The deeds that will guarantee your success as a salesperson are thus:

## 1) <u>TO KNOW THAT YOU CAN DO IT</u>:

✓ **MENTALLY ENVISION THE BEGINNING AND THE END.**

To know that you can do what you desire is a mental determination that fuels your ability to accomplish it. All successful deeds first start with a thought that it can be done. Your conscious mind is the instrument to use to fuel your subconscious mind with successful thoughts. How? Repetitiously implant your conscious mind with words such as "I can..." or "I am..." to let your subconscious mind be aware that you are trying to believe something. Once your subconscious mind becomes aware, then this means that you are successfully beginning to believe in what you're saying or thinking.

   Belief in yourself is the key that will overcome any obstacle. Change your perception if this is not the case at present. Imagine yourself at the top. Vision yourself at the front of the line. See yourself achieving your goals. Have sweet dreams.

   Use your mind and your mouth as the instruments that will set the poetry in motion. Whatever you desire to accomplish, think that you can do it, say that you can do it, repeat to yourself constantly that you can do it, believe that you can do it, and then it shall be done. Belief in yourself is what will make your world a wonderful place.

## 2) <u>TO BE PERSISTENT</u>:

✓ **PHYSICALLY GO ABOUT ACCOMPLISHING THE BEGINNING AND THE END.**

Persistency is doing whatever is necessary to get your prospects to hang around long enough to listen to you. Persistency means you're not going to take "no" for an answer. Persistency means you're in control, and you know it. Consider their rejection as the first step to your success. Consider it as the first and natural reaction from a prospect who does not know what they want or what is best for them. Therefore, consider rejection as a good thing because it gives you an opportunity to work your magic.

   Anyone who practices persistency is bound to be successful in anything they do. Remember, the average prospect will say "no" at least three times before they give in to your offer. So you must be persistent at least four times before giving in to their rejection. Remember, you're in control, though they may think that they are – which is exactly what you want them to think. Don't give up easily. They will actually admire you for it.

## 3) <u>TO DO WHATEVER YOU NEED TO DO TO GET THE PROSPECT(S) TO LIKE YOU</u>:

✓ **THE CHANNEL THAT WILL HELP YOU TO ACCOMPLISH THE BEGINNING AND THE END.**

You cannot get someone to listen to you if they don't like you. Your rapport with the prospect is the core that will get you into their heart.

- ✓ Smile at them
- ✓ Call them by their first name if you have their permission
- ✓ Use the word *you*, referring to them, to show them what you can do for them
- ✓ Shake their hand
- ✓ Mirror their body language
- ✓ Use the same key words they use
- ✓ Listen to them
- ✓ Empathize with them
- ✓ Be yourself and feel relaxed around them
- ✓ Be at ease so they too may be at ease
- ✓ Use the word "because" for every question they ask or for every reason you may give
- ✓ Compliment them
- ✓ Look for common ground
- ✓ Imitate their breathing pattern
- ✓ Say "yes" if they offer you something to drink; exercise caution if necessary
- ✓ Capture their attention by being enthusiastic about what you're offering them
- ✓ Use your hands to demonstrate enthusiasm
- ✓ Introduce your offer with a powerful statement that immediately shows them the benefit
- ✓ Follow the advice that will overcome their objections

❖

These are the three wise deeds that will guarantee your success as a salesperson.

# Topic 41

---

## YOUR ENTHUSIASM IS WHAT WILL GET THEIR ATTENTION

*Nothing great was ever achieved without enthusiasm.*
*- Ralph Waldo Emerson*

If enthusiasm had a voice, this is how it would speak: "You will not believe what I have here to show you!"

Enthusiasm is feeling or showing excitement or strong interest in something. In sales, enthusiasm is the feeling of pride towards your product or service and the excitement of wanting to let others know about and experience it.

You should not come across more enthusiastically than that which is natural for you. Sales involves a degree of acting, and if you can't act the part well, then don't over do it. Practice enthusiasm and then you will suddenly find enthusiasm practicing you.

If you approach or are approached by a prospect who completely lacks enthusiasm, then starting off acting overly excited would be a mistake. Remember, you want to mirror a prospect's behavior and empathize with them. If they lack enthusiasm then you must restrain your enthusiasm and act like them, while keeping at the back of your mind that at some point you're going to have to spark their interest and get them excited.

Your hands can be used to enhance your aura of enthusiasm. Use your hands and arms to demonstrate your enthusiasm towards your product. Let the prospect see your open palms, signaling that you are an open person. Use your hands to make signs and symbols while demonstrating the value of your product.

Sales involves a degree of acting, and enthusiasm for your product is a part of that act. Your product is depending on you to make it look good.

Your service is counting on you to brag about all its fine features and appealing benefits. Then strive not to let them down. But use all your energy, as it would be natural for you to use, to demonstrate the goodness of your services. Turn that which is not exciting into something breathtaking by adding the salt of your enthusiasm. Show the sizzle of the platter to add more flavor to the steak. Transform a beat-up Ford Escort into a dazzling BMW. Make something that is boring into the glitz and glamour of Hollywood with the wave of your magic wand.

Enthusiasm is very contagious, and when you show it, others will naturally want to be a part of the excitement. People hate being left out of anything that's good. This is why it is important to always try your best to use a high level of enthusiasm if conditions permit it. *Your ultimate goal is to spark enthusiasm within the prospect, even if they are resisting it.* You may start slowly, to then build your way up. Your prospect will only be enthusiastic about something if you yourself seem to be enthusiastic about it as well. Nothing great has ever been accomplished without enthusiasm.

In the art of persuasion, enthusiasm can be used as a very effective tool. Enthusiasm helps to changes minds and assists in the process of persuasion. Enthusiasm gives life to that which is non-living. Enthusiasm brightens up a day. Enthusiasm causes waterfalls. Enthusiasm forces its way through the narrowest of spaces. With enthusiasm as your clothing, you will be in the spotlight of your surroundings. Enthusiasm is what makes the world go round.

# Topic 42

---

## CLEAR YOUR MIND TO INFLUENCE OTHERS BETTER

*The sky is the daily bread of the eyes.*
*- Ralph Waldo Emerson*

Whatever may have happened to you in the past, whatever struggles you've faced, whatever obstacle or difficulty you had to confront, if it wasn't a good experience for you, then *forget* about it! Rejuvenate your mind. Give yourself the opportunity to start anew. You owe it to yourself.

Just as the sky is blue, so must your mind be clear, and your thoughts as soft as the clouds. Whenever you're having trouble thinking or solving problems or you find yourself burdened down with too much pressure, look up to the sky to renew your thoughts. No problem is ever too great or too difficult for our universe to handle. Look up to remind yourself of this, like a rainbow reminds us of a promise, that we shall never see the great flood again. Look up to the sky for help and as a reminder that your problems can never be too large.

Look up to the blue sky when times become difficult or when problems seem too much to bear, and let that be a promise unto yourself that all problems can and will be solved.

Look up to the sky to remind yourself of peace and bliss when there is nothing but burdens and troubles below. Let it show you that there is always a way out of every serious situation and that there is always peace after life's struggles, storms and burdens.

When you're not making your sales goals and you feel that sense of hopelessness coming upon you, look up because hope is blue – and our sky is a deep roof of hope over our heads.

If you feel as though you can't take it anymore and there's no way out, enchant your mind once again by looking up and by remembering the good things in life; and that good will triumph over evil.

Remember, always, that no problem is ever too difficult to solve and no trial or test too tough to pass. Remember that the deep blue sky of hope is looking out for you.

Open your mind and let it show you the path. Erase all the negativities, worries, stresses and struggles, tension, hatred and all the hopelessness, and look up because our sky reminds us of the hope that is always there. As long as there's the wonder of the above, and as long as the sun continues to shine, there will always be hope for you and me. So let us look up.

## Don't be negative:

In reference to your prospects, remember to look at each one of them without malice, without prejudice (any form of pre-conceived notions), and with a clear mind. Give each one of them a chance to experience the positive you, and you will find them giving you a chance to experience the positive them. Be inviting, and you will find them letting you into their hearts. Be friendly, and you will find yourself a new friend. Whatever you do, approach each and every one of your prospects with a clear blue thought, that is as soft as the clouds, without any form of negativity; and they will respond kindly to you. They will feel your positive charge and will want to do business with you. But if your vibe is negative, they will flee from you like sheep from wolves.

❖

So remember to always think clear – the color blue – and you will find yourself in the midst of unprecedented sales and success.

# Topic 43

---

## WHATEVER YOU SAY OR DO, DON'T COME ACROSS AS A SALESPERSON

*The secret of success in society is a certain heartiness and sympathy.*
  *- Ralph Waldo Emerson*

Prospects don't like to be sold – they'd rather buy according to what they believe to be "their own will." If you can get the prospect to look at you more as an advisor, a friendly neighbor or a buddy, then you'll see your sales numbers fly through the roof.

### Selling is simply a conversation.

Pay attention to the way you speak with prospects. Listen to your tone and the words you use. Avoid the words and tone that one would typically expect from a salesperson. Talk with the prospect as you would a close friend. Have a conversation with them as opposed to a presentation. Selling is really all about building relationships.

Chitchat with your prospects as opposed to presenting a sales pitch. See them more as a pal or a relative, as opposed to a stranger. Change their title from "prospect" to something else, like "buddy," who you would like to hang out with at a bar or beach or party, and then you'll suddenly see how quickly they will warm up to you.

You won't be able to delete your salesperson vibe one hundred percent, but don't worry because that's what you really are. Just try to do your best not to let the prospect see it.

Change your presentation if your current pitch sounds too sales-like. Become a buddy who likes to chitchat rather than a salesperson who wants to sell.

Your best customers are those who never realize they are being sold. Keep in mind that as a salesperson your job is not just to make sales, but to actually make a difference in people's lives. You're not here just to make a profit; you're here to make it profitable for everyone, including yourself, and your *buddy* formerly known as *prospect*. You're here to assist in whatever way you can to make life easier for your customers, and consequently yourself.

Change your title from salesperson to "assistant" or "the better provider" or "the friendly neighbor" or "the concerned relative." Your job is not to sell to people, your job is to let as many people as possible know you have something *great* that you want them to know about and that you're going to give them, even if they resist it with a "No, thank you." Why? Simply because you're "the concerned citizen."

Be real. Be frank. Be free. Be whatever you need to be to let the prospect know that you're there for them, and not only for yourself. (Then find out what they're doing this weekend.)

# Topic 44

---

## CHANGE YOUR PERCEPTION TO IMPROVE YOUR SELLING

*The more you reason the less you create.*
  *- Raymond Chandler*

If you are not finding success in your efforts, whatever they may be, then it means that something about your thought process is wrong; and your perception is incorrect. To change failure or lack of progress into success, you must change your perception.

It's human nature to be afraid of change. We often become comfortable with what we have, even though it may need to be changed. In the same manner, we are usually comfortable with the way we think, even if it's wrong. In order to change your perception, you must first see the need to change, and then actually want to change. After that, everything else is relatively easy; you'll be on the road leading towards a new pathway to success.

If you are not making your sales numbers, or if your sales performance is not where it should be, then this means that you are doing something wrong, which comes from the fact that you are thinking something wrong, which comes from the fact that something about your perception is wrong. In order to correct this wrong, you must correct the core of the problem, by changing and correcting your perception.

The bottom line is this: if something you're doing or thinking is not working for you, then try something else. If one method doesn't work, then try another one. If you don't know what will work then keep on changing your actions until you find something that finally works for you. Use the method of trial and error if you're having difficulty uncovering the core of the problem. It is okay to fail if your determination is to find the path to success. As long as you're willing to change, and as long as you're willing to find what is successful, then success will ensure that you find it. Success will find you while you're still looking for it. Why? Success likes the company of those who at least put out the effort to try.

This is the biggest problem in changing your perception: you may not know what it is about your perception that needs changing. In fact, what may need changing the most might be what you consider to be the absolute right way of thinking. It may be natural for you to think this way, being that you have been thinking this way for a very long time; maybe ever since your earliest memories.

The core to finding out if your perception is correct is to challenge those parts of your perception that you see absolutely nothing wrong with. If it stands the test of time after a real test, then consider retesting it again to make sure. If it doesn't stand up to scrutiny, then realize this: you've just discovered something many people have never considered, and that in itself will make you one of the most successful people in the world.

# Topic 45

---

## DISCOVER THE METHOD TO ENJOY WHAT YOU DO, DAY-BY-DAY

*The greater the difficulty, the more glory in surmounting it.*
*- Epicurus*

You can only enjoy what you do if you have a desire for what you do. *Like* equals desire. Desire and like go hand in hand.

Desire is the degree of how much you want to do something. Desire is a spark that sets the fuel on fire. Desire is a hunger and thirst. Desire is a curiosity searching for satisfaction. Satisfaction comes from the fact that you have filled the hole that was empty. Satisfaction comes from the accomplishment of a basic want.

Desire also involves pain. Pain can be enjoyable if it leads to something satisfying in the end. That is why fit bodies like to work their muscles until it hurts; because the end result produces a picture perfect image. (You cannot make diamonds without pressure.) Many things that are beautiful were produced from something that was ugly. And this is what makes desire pleasurable – because there is a reward and a feeling of satisfaction and accomplishment at the end of the tunnel.

Selling is not easy in the eyes of many, and that is what makes it so desirable to those who have mastered it. They have become the selected few because they had at least put out the effort to endure the pain. And the pain was not really pain, it was pleasure because at the end of pain is pleasure.

Anything you contemplate in this life that has something to do with being successful usually involves some type of pain. But that pain is not pain if you keep your eyes on the rewards that come after the pain. So prepare yourself to enjoy the pain and you will succeed.

However, it all starts with a spark – a spark of desire. Once you discover desire for what you are aiming for, or should be aiming for, you have already achieved one foot in the door. Desire will make things much easier for you. Desire will speed up the process. Desire will make you endure, and maybe even LIKE the pain. For the pain makes the end results so much more pleasurable. The pain increases the pleasure. One does not know what is sweet until they have tasted that which is sour. One does not know what is beautiful until they have experienced that which is ugly. So enjoy the pain and feel the pleasure.

Find a way to enjoy Sales everyday. Enjoy the pains of selling, and feel the explosive pleasure at the end. Pain is not the end unless you quit half way. Pain leads to pleasure if you follow it all the way.

Don't be afraid of the difficulties of selling and of the cold and unhappy days because those difficult, cold and unhappy days will become nothing but a bunch of old stories after you have endured the pain. Success is waiting for you at the end of the day.

Enjoy the pain and feel the pleasure because that is what leads to success. Make up your mind that life is not easy, and neither is selling. Brace yourself that you may not have enough clothing to cover you in the cold, wintry days of Sales. Prepare yourself that you will not have enough cool breezes for the hot, humid days on the road track of your endeavor. So make up your mind to enjoy the pain. Pain is not pain if you are mentally prepared for it. Pain is pleasure to those who know and understand it. Let pain be your motivation that guides you towards the road to success. Let your growling stomach inspire you to work harder to eat the filet mignon when you have endured the life of the sales man or woman. Make up your mind, and you shall discover the methods that lead to success if you endure the pain. There is truly a method and a way for you to enjoy what you do, each and every day. Put your desire on cruise control, and enjoy the pain.

# Topic 46

## THE WAY YOU HANDLE REJECTION WILL DETERMINE WHETHER OR NOT SALES IS FOR YOU

*Things turn out best for people who make the best of the way things turn out.*
  *- Anonymous*

It's important to realize that sales will not always be a nice, easygoing job. You will sometimes come across very rude, inconsiderate and disrespectful people. There will be days when you will encounter many very distasteful people. How you handle these people and their rejections will determine if you are suited for the challenges of sales.

Sales can be a tough job, especially if you don't know how to handle rejection; and if you're not making your sales numbers or commission. It can seem like an unrewarding job at times and you may feel under-appreciated. The way you deal with these situations and feelings will determine your level of comfort and security in your job.

To be a successful salesperson you must learn to deal with rejections properly and promptly. The way to deal with rejection is to never take any form of rejection personally. If you do, then you are harming no one but yourself. You must create within your mind a space specifically for those occasions when you're feeling under-appreciated and devalued. Create a dumping site within your mind that processes and dumps the trash of inconsiderate, disrespectful and rude people. You must turn these people's actions and behavior into a harmless substance by adding a degree of your determination, thereby not allowing them to get to you. You must mix their ignorance with your understanding to create a substance that is less potent.

Allow this less potent substance to deflate itself and evaporate from your mind, body and soul. See it evaporate and disappear into the mist of the atmosphere as it leaves.

If you don't learn how to handle rejection then you will *not* be successful in sales. However once you know how to turn rejection into something that makes you stronger and sting less, then *nothing* will stop you from reaching your goals. Only YOU can stop YOU from reaching your goal. You are the biggest rejection that you will have to overcome. Once you do that then all other rejections are futile, like mist disappearing in the wind.

Sales can be hard if you let the rejection factor get to you. You must not harbor any rejections; instead you must find a way to turn them into something humorous. Yes, something that makes you laugh. Laugh it off and it will not leave an imprint on your psyche. If the prospect's rude behavior offended you then turn it into a joke. Have fun with sales and have fun with rejections because they are a part of sales. Every rejection brings you closer to a sale. And then when you're cashing those large checks, you will be the last one laughing all the way to the bank. She who laughs lasts laughs best. Life is a game and selling is fun, so enjoy it and play on.

# Topic 47

---

## DISCOVER THE SIMPLE METHOD OF CHANGING MINDS

*We don't know who first discovered water, but we can be sure that it wasn't a fish.*
   *- Howard Gossage*

You can change a prospect's mind by using either of these two methods:

### 1. Bring them down to your level
### 2. Bring them up to your level

You will need to judge and decide which method you are going to use based on your assessment of the prospect.

Most people's thought patterns are based on nothing more than opinions. Opinions are inherently weak and can be obliterated by the slightest wind that challenges it. Most people argue what they like or dislike based on their weak points of view. If you challenge their opinions they will often not stand up to scrutiny.

Opinions are not facts or truths, and most people know that. In reality, most people like it when their weak opinions are challenged because they inevitably prefer facts over feelings.

When a prospect gives a reason why they like or dislike something, they are basing it on their opinions. Opinions are always open for debate. If a prospect insists they dislike something, as a salesperson, you shouldn't let that intimidate you because opinions can change if you challenge them. When a prospect expresses their dislike for something, ask them why. Based on their weak or seemingly strong reasoning, decide how you are going to handle your presentation in order to obliterate their thought pattern and change their flawed way of thinking.

An opinion is simply a choice based on how it makes the person feel. An opinion is simply a choice that someone chooses out of a bunch of choices. An opinion can be as simple as a choice of color that a prospect chooses based on the selection that are available. An opinion can change color like an octopus can change shape. Opinions are one of the most unstable and inconsistent aspects of one's thoughts. Therefore, an opinion can be easily changed if put to the test, especially if that test involves hardcore facts.

If you want to change someone's mindset, consider using the method of bringing them down to your level, or bringing them up to your level.

## 1) Bring them down to your level:

If your prospect is resisting you by imposing their defensive wall of opinions, you may bring them down to your level. Start by admitting that you may not know much, but you have this gut feeling that your suggestion is better for them. If your reasoning of why they should see things your way is not based on fact, then use your own personal instinct over fact. For example, if the prospect thinks they shouldn't spend more money for something, then use a method that allows them to see through your eyes. "I don't believe you should be paying a penny more than what you're paying now, but I have a gut instinct that you will feel happier if you were to give it a try. Why don't you try something newer, better and different, and see what happens? You don't have anything to lose and you may just realize what you've been missing out on."

## 2) Bring them up to your level:

If a prospect is stating opinions that are not accurate or facts that are weak, then it is time to bring them up to your level. For example, if a prospect is looking for a truck that has a two-wheel drive system, which is less expensive than a truck with a four-wheel drive system, try persuading the prospect as follows: "Even though it is true that a two-wheel drive truck is cheaper, you can't do much with a two-wheel drive truck. Trucks were meant to be rough and tough four-wheel drive vehicles. What happens when you want to resell a two-wheel drive truck? Who will want to buy your two-wheel drive truck five years from now? Are you thinking for the future, Richard?"

Changing minds is as simple as changing opinions. Prospects' opinions are simply based on choices they had available at a certain point in time, or the first choice that came to mind, and they kept it. They also develop opinions based on the way it makes them feel or their limited knowledge of the subject. Your task is to present them with a new idea, a new way of thinking and a new feeling. Changing minds may not be as difficult as you may have thought. Be sure to change your *weak* opinion on that.

# Topic 48

## WHY THIS BOOK CAN BE DANGEROUS

*Master books, but do not let them master you. Read to live, not live to read.*
  *- Edward Bulwer-Lytton*

This book can be dangerous for the same reason why any self-improvement book can be dangerous – your dependency on it. Remember, all books have a front cover and a back, which means there are limitations. However a person's imagination has no end. A book is only the tip of the iceberg to what the realms of your imagination can do in addition to the book.

You never want to use a book to guide you through what you ought to be doing, but only as a reference to what you should already be doing. Make your self-improvement book proud of you by not only doing what it says, but by extending yourself and by doing more than what it says. Don't let the book be your guide to living life, but rather a reference guide to the life you are already living.

Your imagination has no limits, and this book is only a small guide to the universe of your imagination and goals that are ready to be explored and achieved by you.

*The Method Of Selling* is only a guide to get you started. You are the vehicle that will drive your way to success. Let it be that one day, you do not become a student of this book, but a mentor who could teach even this book those things that it may be lacking. From this book, may your imagination and the success that you will be really living write many more books in the hearts of those who see your deeds and know your ways as an example for all to follow.

You are an evolving creature, changing for either the better or the worse each second. You are a flowing body of water, running wild and enthusiastic in the stream of life. You are an endless resource for knowledge and self-improvement. But this book is only able to provide a miniscule amount of the great abundance of wealth, happiness and success that is yet to be achieved each day within our hearts and minds.

So never limit yourself, and know that you are a moving soul, constantly changing to suit your environment, and constantly shedding the old, and becoming the new. You are success in motion, capable of greater and greater deeds. Let this book be only a guide to the success that you are already experiencing.

But this book does serve its purpose. It will not be dangerous if you look at it and use it in the right way. Each time you read it you will discover something new, with the help of your creative imagination. It will serve as a reference guide to the wealthy, healthy and successful life that you are striving for and forging ahead each day to live. This is a feel-good book. It makes you feel good knowing that what you're doing is here in writing. It makes you feel secure to know that you are on the right track, and your efforts are not in vain. It gives you hope that every time you should fall, you'll always have a support by your side to pick you right back up. Enjoy, use and live it each and every day of your life.

# Topic 49

---

## KNOW YOUR PRODUCT OR SERVICE LIKE THE BACK OF YOUR HAND

*Knowledge is power.*
*- Francis Bacon*

Make it a point to put in the effort to learn at least ten main features about each product or service, ten main benefits about those features; and ten main attributes that your product or service has above the competition.

Learn at least ten features and ten benefits of your competition that may be considered "better" than your product or service. Investigate what is causing your prospects to fish on the other side of the pond.

Examine your product or service and figure out what are the ten main points of interest most people look for when considering them. For example, if you are selling shoes, then find the ten main reasons why customers love and buy your shoes.

It is also important to examine your product or service to discover the ten main reasons why prospects don't buy them and betray you by devoting their purchase to Judas, your competition.

Sales involves some aspects of marketing. A good salesperson will take polls on what people like most about their product or service and keep this record at the forefront of their minds.

Marketing involves finding out what people like and why they like it. The purpose of marketing is to discover a way to bring prospective buyers to your product or service. Therefore, it is always wise for you to extend your sales title by incorporating marketing strategies as well. Learn the ten best things about your product or service that turned on previous buyers; and learn the ten things that turned them off as well.

164

This will give you an edge when dealing with prospects who, for example, put up their "smoke screens" by not revealing what they are looking for or what turns them on about your product or service.

Prospects admire salespeople who are knowledgeable. They appreciate salespeople who take the time to learn about what they're selling. It makes them feel secure knowing that they are doing business with someone who knows what they are doing.

Unless you are new to the company, you should be very well versed and knowledgeable about what you're selling. If you are not, then you may be giving your product or service a bad name. Do your company, your prospects and yourself a favor, and know your products or services like the back of your hand.

Selling is such a vast universe of information that it is impossible to ever know everything. It would be unwise for you to say something like, "I already know that," because information presented can always open up a new awareness within you at any given time. You are never too big to learn, or re-learn over and over again what you already know. Any opportunity you get to learn something new in sales, or re-learn something that you already know, should always be looked upon as an opportunity of a lifetime because that little extra information can increase your selling ability super extra.

# Topic 50

## ANYBODY CAN LEARN THE METHOD OF SELLING AND SUCCEED IN IT

*Nothing is difficult to those who have the will.*
*- Motto of the Dutch Poets' Society*

The bottom line to selling is to tighten *your* ability to persuade others to listen and comply. The core point to succeed in Sales is to believe that you can do it, and know that you are the best man or woman for the job at hand. Once you can absorb this notion – that you can do it – then everything else will fall into place quite easily. Belief in yourself is the foundation that will build a stable relationship between you and the method of selling. If you don't practice believing in yourself, then the foundation will be an unstable one – ready to fall apart when the big bad wolf huffs and puffs and blows your house down.

Anybody can learn the method of selling because it's easy if you make it easy on yourself. It will only be hard if you make it hard for yourself. If you think you can do it, then you're right. However, if you think you can't do it, then you'll also be right. The key to your success will depend on which right side you want to be on.

You sold yourself this morning on the notion that you needed to wake up and accomplish what you needed to do. You sold yourself on that notion because you thought you had to, or else, you knew there might have been consequences if you didn't sell yourself on that notion. If you practice this concept in the same manner when you're trying to sell something, then you will most likely be one of the greatest salespeople in the world. However you might say that you don't need to be the greatest salesperson in the world. That's okay too. Just be the greatest salesperson in your accomplished mind.

166

If you can breathe then you can sell. In fact, selling is a necessity to survive. Wherever you're at right now in life is a direct result of your selling ability. You can improve your selling by just accelerating your desire. Your desire and willpower will produce an outstanding output if you acquire a little more of each.

Selling is easy if you make it easy on yourself. Look at the bright side of selling and you will see the light that leads to you successful selling. Look at the dark side, and you will stumble about in the dark, not knowing where you are going. So it all depends on how you look at it, or not look at it.

You can achieve in Sales because you already are a salesperson. All you need to do is sharpen your Sales blades. Make the rough edges smooth by ironing your sense to sell. Picture yourself selling rather than seeing yourself walking away from sales. Keep your head up high rather than wallowing in the gutters.

Success is yours if you extend your hand to take it. Prospects are your calling if you don't plug up your ears with cotton wool. Greatness is yours if you don't hide under a table.

You will achieve at selling if selling achieves its way into your heart. There is *nothing* you cannot do if your willpower is to do it. And your desire will propel you to move forward. Proceed on the road of Sales, and endure and you shall succeed. The world of selling is your abode if you think, sleep and eat it.

# Topic 51

## YOUR WILLPOWER HAS TO BE STRONGER THAN THE PROSPECT'S

*The will to conquer is the first condition of victory.*
*- Marshal Ferdinand Foch*

Every time you perform a sales presentation with a prospect, a sale will always be made. It's either you are going to make a sale with this prospect, or the prospect is going to sell you a reason why they can't buy from you. Your willpower has to be stronger than the prospect's willpower if you intend to win the discourse. Your reason why they should buy from you must be stronger than their will to shrug you off.

Your willpower has to be stronger than the willpower of the prospect if you intend to win. But it does not have to be much stronger. Willpower that is stronger only by the size of a pinhead is all the willpower you need to overcome the prospect's objections. If the prospect's willpower weighs 30 pounds, and your willpower is 30.01 pounds, then you win. If the prospect's willpower is 12 inches long and yours is 12.01 inches, then you win again. As long as your willpower is just a miniscule amount greater than the prospect's, then you will always turn out to be the victor.

Willpower is determination as determination is the strength to carry on and win. Your willpower aims to win. It does not believe in defeat or retreat. The situation has to be a dire one before the likes of willpower decides to take a break. Make sure you're in good health when the button of willpower turns itself on with a green light because willpower aims to stay up all night long if need be.

Every time you fail to achieve a sale with a prospect, always remember and know that the reason why you failed was because your willpower was weaker than that of the prospect's. Build up your willpower to maximum strength if you desire to overcome the prospect's willpower. Take your willpower to the gym, and pump those muscles back up to optimum performance. Use the protein shake called desire to add strength to your willpower. Don't quit 'til you get it right. Don't give up 'til your muscles are sore and ached. Use every bit of effort that you have to build up that willpower to where it needs to be. Practice it everyday. Make it a habit, and like it. (From pain comes pleasure.)

The day you find a pattern whereby you're winning over your prospects to a stable degree, then know that you have achieved the willpower level you were looking for. Your willpower will do wonders for you if you exercise it right. If you feed your willpower with the right nutrients it will produce a successful track record for you that is hard to beat. Your willpower is stronger than you, and it will treat you right if you feed it right.

You need not worry about whether or not you're going to win over your prospects if your willpower is indeed properly maintained. Maintain your willpower by keeping it in tiptop shape, ready, waiting and willing to take on whatever challenges life has to offer. Your willpower fears nothing but that which is necessary to fear.

With a strong willpower, the state called worry does not exist. Anxiety or uncertainty has no room in the house that is occupied by the tenant named willpower. Fear is nothing but a myth in the eyes of willpower unless that fear can prove itself otherwise.

The house of willpower is kept clean and secure. A storm will not disturb the sleep of willpower. High winds will not awaken the eyes of willpower from a sweet dream. Only the aroma of a fresh brew of coffee will disturb the sleep of willpower as the dawn of the early morning rises. Thus, arise yourself, and awaken your mind to a newer and stronger form of willpower!

# Topic 52

## ALWAYS KEEP AT THE FRONT OF YOUR MIND WHY YOUR PROSPECTS SHOULD BUY FROM YOU

*Take away the cause, and the effect ceases.*
        *- Miguel de Cervantes*

The question every prospect is going to always be asking themselves is "What's in it for me?" or the acronym WIIFM. You must be prepared with answers and reasons why the prospect should buy from you. You must be able to convince and persuade your prospect that it is better for them to have what you have to offer them than to not have it. You must clearly state the reason why they should and the void they will get if they don't claim *their* product or service.

Always keep at the front of your mind why your prospect should buy from you because they are keeping such thoughts at the front of theirs. Always remember to press the refresh button everyday as to what you are offering and why. Always remember to renew your thoughts and reasoning about what makes your product or service so special. Always be ready to give a reason without thinking about why you're selling what you're selling.

People buy things, ideas and services because it assists in solving their problems. What problems are you solving for the prospect who buys your product or service? If you don't have an answer without thinking about it, then you are not ready to sell anything to anyone. If you must stop and think why you're selling what you're selling, then that means you lack the passion that is necessary to sell it. *If there is no passion, then there is no sale – without passion there is no convincing.* You need the type of passion that motivates you to achieve your goals. And the only way to develop that passion is to know what you are doing and why. If you do not know what you are doing and why, then your prospect, too, will not know what you are doing and why. A prospect will sense when a salesperson knows what they are doing and can feel their passion. A salesperson with passion is on a mission – to solve problems.

Just as you know that one plus one equals two, so should you know why your prospects should buy from you. If you don't know why then write down the reasons a hundred times on paper until you get it. Do not dare say, "Huh?" to a prospect who asks you what makes your product so much better than what they have now.

What made you decide to wear the clothing you're wearing now? Is it because you like the color, or the style, or the price they cost, or the way they make you feel, or the quality, or the way they make you look? For the same reason that makes you like the things you bought – or that which was given to you – so must you have an answer for the things you sell.

Prospects have the same taste as you – they want the best, and they want it for the cheapest price possible. Don't shortchange your prospects by being unprepared.

It is not the fine features of your product or service that is going to be the finger that pushes your prospects' hot button, but rather it is the *benefits* to these features that will make your prospects' mouths water and their minds wonder to the state of owning what they do not have yet; that which you're about to give them. Demonstrate to your prospect how what you have to sell is going to fit into their life. Show them how it's going to fit into their unique family structure. Let them feel themselves fitting into the design of your product or service. Let them know what they can do and how they can do it with your product or service. Let them see how your product or service is going to save them time and money. Show them how it benefits them health-wise. Say to your prospect, "This product has a feature whereby you press this help button, and you will get all the information you need. So the benefit to you would be that help is always available at the click of a button. You will never have to put up with the headache of trying to understand something you don't know. Help is always there at the click of a button."

# Topic 53

---

## MENTALLY ENVISION IT STEP-BY-STEP

*Vision is the art of seeing things invisible.*
    *- Jonathan Swift*

When you rise up off your seat or bend your knee to lift your foot after reading this or another topic you will go and do something else, and you will most likely succeed in it. Why? You will succeed merely because you envisioned it. Whether it is going to the refrigerator for a glass of water or walking towards your car to take a ride somewhere, you will most likely achieve it because you envisioned it. You had a sense of direction as to where you will be going and what you will be doing. It happened in your mind, and so shall it happen in your actions; because you envisioned it.

In the same manner, if you want to be successful with anything in life, you must envision it in your mind first. The task must be considered done with the keen eyes of your imagination. You must see it as already having happened. If you do not envision what you will be doing, then you will be as one walking among the blind. Create a picture in motion of what you plan to achieve, or else stumble badly, all the time.

If you want to be successful in sales, then envision sales being successful in you. Let your imagination go wild. Let it dream of things that are not, but that are going to be with the powerful eye of your imagination.

Envision yourself having success. See yourself in the surroundings that you want to be in. Look at yourself traveling on the pathway of freedom. Don't be afraid to use your imagination to create that which is not because your imagination will turn that which is not into that which is. A city is built out of the imagination of those who fashioned it.

If you hope to be a successful salesperson, then see yourself busy and working hard. See yourself making appointments non-stop. See customers streaming towards you, shaking your hand and smiling at you. See yourself receiving calls to the point where you can't keep up with them. See yourself giving people what they want. See yourself persuading people to follow your lead. See your customers bringing customers to you. See yourself making people laugh. See yourself making prospects happy. See yourself stacking up cash in your savings account. See yourself enjoying what you do. See yourself being in the career of your dreams. Do all this first, and you will succeed. (Seeing is truly believing.)

Don't be afraid to get carried away with your imagination, or else your imagination will carry itself away from you. *Crazy* is the name of your imagination. Don't be afraid to go wild and have fanciful thoughts because that's just what your imagination is all about. Your imagination thrives in madness. And you are your imagination.

All the great people of the world are great because they went along with the lunacy of their imagination. They dreamed incredible dreams, which became reality. But a dream that is mild and without passion will achieve little or no success in the realms of the real world.

So envision success, and success will see you through the tunnel on the other side. Walk in the pathway of success that you have created with your imagination, and you will reduce your chance of stumbling. Trust your thoughts and your imagination, and they will take good care of you like a baby. They will comfort you when you cry, and help you up when you fall. They will be by your side in the good times and bad. They will laugh with you during the good days, and hold your hand when you're feeling down. Trust your thoughts and envision great things and dream great dreams. Follow the pathway that leads to success. Embark on the road that leads to riches. Envision this EVERYDAY, until that dream day becomes your reality. Do these things and success shall be yours.

# Topic 54

---

## FOLLOW THE LAW OF EXPECTATION

*Act as if it were impossible to fail.*
  - *Dorothea Brande*

*To expect* is to look forward to something that you have no doubt will happen. The law of expectation is to feel secure that what you think is going to happen is actually going to happen, with no strings attached.

The mistake that some salespeople make is to weakly hope for something that they fear will not happen. This is not the law of expectation. This is the law of a self-fulfilling prophecy of doubt and insecurity.

If you want to be successful in sales, then your expectation has to be real and concrete. Your expectation should be such that you would still believe in it even if it didn't come through. Your expectation should be even stronger than the outcome itself. Your expectation should be so high that you would have to force yourself to believe that it did not happen, if it actually didn't happen.

Anything other than having a firm expectation is not following the law of expectation. If you doubt your expectation, then you are wishing upon a hopeless cause that will come through only by the *law of accident.*

There is no need to doubt your expectation if you have everything else all figured out. And that everything else is the confidence within you. Your confidence is four pillars of stones, surrounding your great expectation. They are reinforced by steel and will not weaken or fall. They will hold up your expectation safe and secure.

When you are trying to sell something to a prospect, do not hope or wish with one eye closed that they will buy from you. Expect that they will buy from you. Your expectation has a lot to do with the outcome of the prospect's decision to buy from you. If your expectation is weak, then the prospect will pick up on that, and will find a loophole to escape through the insecurities of your weak expectation. But if your expectation is firm, then your prospect is boxed up in the jail of your knowledge that a sale will be made.

Your expectation creates an aura around you. A person who doubts his or her expectation and a person who believes in his or her expectation are two completely different looking people in the eyes of a prospect. A light shines on the one who expects that their effort will produce results, while the one who doubts his expectation is a light bulb about to die out. (Let your light shine before us all.)

If you want to feel firm and secure in sales, then sit as judge in the courtroom of great expectations. Follow the law of expectation, and do not contradict your belief. Make it easy on yourself by not going against yourself. Don't even question yourself. But know and trust yourself, and stand firm in your belief that you will succeed.

The strength of your expectation extends far into the distance. As far as your expectation is, is as far as your success limit is. If your expectation is limitless, then your success will be there right next to it. In general, if you plan to succeed with anything, then you must send your great expectation in front of, and ahead of you. Your expectation will clear the way for you, and make the path easy to travel. (Great riches will be yours.)

Your expectation must be so strong that its presence is as that of another person. Your expectation has a life of its own. Its life is to serve all those who use its law. Its salvation is to turn your wishes and hopes into real things that you can touch and see, and smell.

If your expectation is working properly, then you won't have to do much work because your expectation will negotiate secretly in the minds of those you are trying to convince. If you should be successful in a life as a salesperson, then follow the great law of expectation. Truly expect it, and it shall happen as clear as your vision is. (And the sight of the blind shall be restored!)

# Topic 55

## MAKE YOUR FIRST REQUEST WITHIN SECONDS UPON MEETING YOUR PROSPECT

*Who makes quick use of the moment is a genius of prudence.*
  *- Johann Kaspar Lavater*

Unless you're already caught up in the chitchat mode with your prospect, ask them to do something for you within seconds upon meeting them. If you're on the front steps of their home, for example, you could simply ask them to let you into their home because it's too cold outside; or you could ask them for a glass of water. The reason why you want to do this early on is to subconsciously get them used to doing things for you, so that when you want your biggest request fulfilled– which is to have them buy something from you – they will continue that flow and rhythm of doing things for you.

   You don't want to be obvious in your approach, but subtle. Make a simple request by asking the prospect what time it is, if they're wearing a watch. But be sure you're not wearing a watch if you plan to use this approach.

   You may even ask your prospect not only for things, but ask them complimentary questions as well. Ask them, "Where did you get those beautiful flowers from?"

   The point is that you always want to ask a question to get an answer or a deed fulfilled from the prospect. You want to tap into the boundaries of the prospect's willingness to accommodate you. You want to program the prospect's heart into that of a giving heart. You want the prospect to develop a spirit of sharing their time and energy with you. You want the prospect to think that they will be somehow or someway blessed by their good deeds toward you. And they will be.

But not only that – you want to maintain yourself in the asking mode so that you won't feel out-of-place asking for the sale at the end of your presentation. You want to pave the way smooth so that you can assume the sale as an assumptive close without directly asking for the sale. You probably even want to urge a "yes" out of the prospect without the need to ask. You want to create an atmosphere of giving within the prospect's heart. (Tis the season to be giving.)

And you want to do this all very quickly, starting within seconds of meeting the prospect. You want to train their mind early on that the relationship between both of you is going to be a giving one. And the way to do this is to get them in the mode of saying "yes" to anything as earlier as possible in the presentation.

You also want to let the prospect know that you have something to give to them; that you are not only there to receive. In fact, you want the prospect to know that you have more to give them than they could ever repay you back with. You want to let them know that their needs and wants will more greatly be fulfilled by receiving the gifts and joy you bring. ("Will you be my Santa?")

This is not a joke, but you can joke about it. You want to teach your prospect about being courteous and exhibiting good manners towards you as a salesperson, or else they might just leave you out in the cold. Sometimes prospects don't know that they are being rude or inconsiderate unless you point it out to them. So urge them to develop the giving spirit because their giving spirit will prosper them in ways too great to mention, long after you're gone. Make them want to give, and to give happily unto you. And the relationship between the two of you will blossom like a cherry tree.

# Topic 56

## KEEP IT SHORT AND SWEET

*Let thy speech be short, comprehending much in few words.*
   *- Ecclesiasticus*

*Words should be weighed and not counted.*
   *- Yiddish proverb*

One thing you must always be up to par with is to get your point across quickly. Prospects are not looking for a lecture from you – they are looking for a good reason why they should part from their well-earned dollar unto you. And you better be ready to give them one, if not many.

Be in the habit of using short, sweet sentences that carry powerful messages. Choose words that make up intense sentences. Use phrases that capture the attention of anyone. Use dialogue that awakens the desire and curiosity of your prospects.

There is the possibility of overstating too many facts and benefits to your prospect. A prospect is not necessarily looking for all the features and benefits of your product; rather they are looking for the features and benefits that pertain to them. Overstating too many features and benefits can actually cast a negative light on your product for some prospects. They will ponder whether or not they are making a good choice by getting a product with so many features they probably don't need. They will also wonder if they should purchase something cheaper. To avoid this situation, it is always wise to ask the prospect specifically what they are looking for, and narrow your presentation to those key points that are of interest to them.

Some salespeople speak themselves into the sale and then right back out by refusing to shut up. It is wise and safe to stay focused on the issue at hand; always keeping in mind to tailor your presentation to fit the prospect's needs or wants.

Keep your presentations short, sweet and to the point, or else you may just lose your prospect in all the confusion. Give them key points to remember, and to not forget. Make certain points marinate in the prospect's mind so that their mouth may water for your service. Emphasize certain points by *pausing* after making them, so that they may digest it all the more.

Do not be too wordy in your explanations. Find words that quickly and accurately answer your prospect's questions. Treat your presentations as if you only had five minutes, even though it may take a full two hours to complete.

The last thing you want to do is sound boring in front of your prospect. Use enthusiastic words such as *fast... impressive... dazzling... special... fun... exciting...* Highlight key phrases that will awaken the eyes of your prospect and open their mouth with surprise. Strike a cord with their senses by playing a tune they love.

Tell stories to your prospects, but remember to keep them too short and sweet. And you better make sure that they have a punch line at the end. Give them something to think about – food for thought. Make them remember you for your wild and ludicrous stories – stories that will leave an impression upon them.

Use examples in your presentation where deemed appropriate, but keep these too, short and simple and to the point. Use bright examples that will glare in the prospect's eyes. Temporarily blind them with your amazing and incredible storytelling abilities. Use examples that will make them laugh. Seal the deal with an example of a customer who gave a testimonial about being extremely satisfied with you and your service. Create your own stamp of approval. (Isn't this topic short and sweet?)

# Topic 57

## BE YOURSELF NO MATTER WHAT THAT SELF IS

*Do not wish to be anything but what you are, and try to be that perfectly.*
   *- St. Francis de Sales*

*If I try to be like him, who will be like me?*
   *- Yiddish proverb*

### The true you is "you" with all your strengths and insecurities.

Your prospect is looking for the real you. They do not want to search to find you. They do not want to look inside of you to see you. They want to experience you and your real thoughts and feelings exposed right there in front of them. That is what will make them like you. If you show them an imitation of yourself, they will resent the counterfeit person you are representing. In their eyes, the real you is a blemished diamond. If you pretend to be something or someone that you are not, then they will consider your act and everything else as a cheap sale.

Prospects find it insulting when salespeople are not being honest and straightforward with them. They consider it as an offense. It makes them uncomfortable. Only the true you will make them comfortable. If you are being something or someone other than yourself, the prospect will see through the fake act. They want to know that you can feel as comfortable with them as they should feel with you. They want you to talk with them as if you were their personal right hand man or woman. They want a real relationship.

Even though the real you may have flaws, that too may seem sexy to the prospect who realizes that you are being real and sincere. They want to really know how you feel. They want to really know how you talk.

They want to really know how you think. They want to know that they can sit around a campfire and chitchat with you. They want to know what your insecurities are because they too have insecurities. They do not mind if you are imperfect; in fact, they do not care if you are imperfect. They do not want a *salesperson*; they want a *real-person* who can be open and honest with them.

Prospects like dealing with people who they can trust. And the only way they are going to trust you is to see you as you really are. Even if they are your first prospect ever, they won't mind. They will even like that all the more. They will give you a break. Even some professional salespeople who have been in the business for years, want their prospects to think that *today* is their first day selling. You will actually score more points with many prospects who think that you are inexperienced.

Why do you think men fantasize about female virgins so much? They love the freshness. They love the idea that the woman is not so-called "tainted." They love the idea of being the first. Don't be afraid to show your prospects your vulnerability because they too have vulnerabilities. Everybody has vulnerabilities. The more vulnerable you are the more you remind your prospects of themselves. Why? A prospect often looks at themselves as having the short end of the stick when they are dealing with salespeople. Change their perception by showing them the real you and your vulnerability.

Be yourself with all your prospects and they will think they can tell you anything. They will open up to you when they see your openness towards them. You will have just scored yourself 60 points once a prospect discovers you are being yourself with them. It makes them feel special.

If you have an accent, then don't be ashamed of it. People with accents do very well in sales because prospects trust the vulnerability of such salespeople. Don't be ashamed if you have a handicap, if you stammer or if you don't have any fashion sense. Don't be afraid if you are too tall or too big, if you don't know what you are doing or if you are hard of hearing. Don't be afraid if you are shy and inexperienced. Why? The prospect will love you for your shyness and inexperience. They love your vulnerability and your insecurities. They love you because they know that even though you may hold setbacks, you won't let these setbacks hold you back. And this will encourage them to deal with their own setbacks in much the same way. You will be a role model unto them in ways you may not even understand. Be yourself and you won't go wrong.

# Topic 58

## YOUR EMPATHY TOWARDS THEM IS WHAT WILL DRAW THEM CLOSER TO YOU

*The only gift is a portion of thyself.*
      *- Ralph Waldo Emerson*

*Stop selling. Start helping.*
      *- Zig Ziglar*

Your prospect wants to sense that your desire to assist them is greater than your desire to make a commission. Your prospect wants to know that if you were doing it for free, would you still want to assist them. Your prospect wants to know if you would have come to their party if they had invited you.

Empathy is showing understanding and concern for your prospect's thoughts, feelings and needs. Empathy is listening for the purpose of bettering your prospect's desire. Empathy is stopping what you are doing for someone who you want to do something special for. Empathy is your love of the prospect's company. Empathy is treating the prospect as you would like to be treated. Empathy is taking off your sales hat and looking at the prospect as someone with feelings and concerns, just like yourself. Your prospect is looking for someone who really cares about them. Their search ends when they find that your cause is their yearning. The prospect wants a truthful answer if they were to ask you, "If you were me, what would you do?" The prospect wants to know if you will still remember them five years from now. Your prospect wants to know if they were crying their eyes out two minutes before they saw you, if you would have noticed and asked, "Are you ok?" and "What's wrong?" This is true empathy.

The day a prospect discovers that you truly empathize with their situation, is the day your sales job just became 90 percent easier. A prospect who sees your empathy will open up to you like a long lost relative. They will not hesitate to give you the codes to their most inner desires and weaknesses. Their bank account statement will have your product's name on it.

Follow the rule of treating everybody as you would like to be treated, and all things that you desire will come to you. If you have mastered the calling for empathy, then you do not need to worry about being a salesperson anymore. You will do well just by being a good person.

Your empathy towards your prospect is what will draw them close, and closer to you. A salesperson with empathy does not need to remember how to close a sale. The *empathized* prospect will close it for him or her. Life is well for the person who knows how to empathize with others. (And there shall be no want or need.)

Besides believing in yourself, empathy towards others is probably the next best thing to successful selling. I know of a salesman who remembers the names of all the hundreds of customers he has. Some of them have actually given him the codes to their luxury homes to do his drop-offs when they are not home. I even remember his first name. It's Michael.

You do not need to remember the hundreds of names of your customers, but you better know the name of the prospect who is in front of you right now. And if you have a bad memory, that's what pen and paper is for, right?

There is a certain look in the eyes of someone who empathizes for their prospects and customers – it is the look of caring. It is the look of concern. It is the act of asking questions constantly to understand and precisely match the needs and wants of your prospect.

You could know and practice all the other methods in this book and still not succeed if there is no empathy to your selling. What is the point of selling something to someone if there is no love? The love of others is the root of successful selling.

# Topic 59

## ADDRESS THEIR CONCERNS BEFORE THEY DO

*The most important persuasion tool you have in your entire arsenal is integrity.*
  *- Zig Ziglar*

You must know and be prepared for almost every objection or excuse a prospect can come up with for not wanting to buy your product or service. You must make the effort to inform yourself and know every flaw that exists within your product or service.

The safest way to sell a product is to know its flaws and point them out to the prospect before they see them and point them out to you. If you do this first – before they do – you will have two main advantages on your side:

### 1) They will trust you as a person for pointing out flaws that they did not know or may not have discovered.
And credibility is what turns a salesperson into a prospect's friend.

The prospect will silently thank you in their heart or with a whisper beneath their breath for letting them know things they probably would not have discovered if you didn't point them out to them. In such an instance you would have sold yourself more so than the product. And remember, a typical prospect is going to buy you, as a person, before they buy you, as a product. Sell yourself by showing your trustworthiness and sincerity to all your prospects.

## 2) You will lessen the potency of the flaw by pointing it out first.

By pointing it out first, the prospect's objection to that flaw in your product or service will seem miniscule when it comes out of their mouth. That flaw will lose its potency if you point it out before your prospect gets a hand on it.

In addition to pointing out the flaw, your next move would be to mitigate the flaw. You may say something like, "This vacuum cleaner may look big and clumsy, but that's because it carries such a powerful motor, and they couldn't find a way to make it any smaller."

If you can give a reasonable argument for your product's or service's flaw(s) then you have gained yourself another 20 points.

Many prospects will already know the flaw your product or service contains even before you point it out to them. But just by the mere fact that you actually pointed it out to them, and still feel and show confidence in your product speaks for itself. *"Why would a salesperson still be enthusiastic about selling a product that he or she knows has flaws?"* is the question the prospect is asking themselves. And they will answer their own question by saying, "Maybe because the flaw is insignificant compared to the benefits of this service? Maybe the benefits outweigh the flaw(s)?"

What is the best time to point out a flaw in your service or product? You should do so after demonstrating the benefits to your prospect. Give them the good news first, then the bad after, and then reinforce the good news again with the power word "however." Follow this pattern each time you have a flaw to disclose about what you are selling.

Do not point out your product's/service's flaws in consecutive order, one right after the next, if there are more than two flaws. Instead, separate each flaw by describing a significant benefit of your service to the prospect first. Use your discretion. And if the prospect manages to bring up the flaw before you get a chance to address it, then don't worry – just agree with them, with a beneficial strategy next in line.

The product or service you are trying to sell may contain major flaws. If you do not believe in the product you are selling, or if your notion is that the flaw exceeds the benefits, then you need to consider changing the product line you are selling. A salesperson must believe in the product he or she is selling or else they will not seem convincing when selling it. It can be easy for a prospect to detect whether or not a salesperson is really interested in the product or service he or she is selling. So be sure to stick with products or services that you believe in. Otherwise you may have to find yourself another sales job that you're really interested in.

# Topic 60

---

## LET THEM IMAGINE THAT IT IS THEIRS ALREADY

*The lightning spark of thought generated in the solitary mind awakens its likeness in another mind.*

*- Thomas Carlyle*

Temporarily give each prospect your service or product for free. Let them imagine that it is theirs for a minute. Give them time to think and bond with what you have to sell. Make them feel what it's like to have it. And if they object, remind them what it's going to be like without it.

You want to fill a gap in the prospect's life by making them want what you have. And you want to create a gap in their heart by having to take away what they've had the chance to keep. Refrain from making your presentation as them not wanting it, but as you not wanting to take it away from them.

Proclaim to your prospect that what you have to sell them was theirs from the very beginning. Show them how it fits them like a glove. Show them how it complements them as a person. Let them see how it fits in with their intellect. Demonstrate to them that purchasing your product or service will be their wisest decision of the week. Make them not want to leave home without owning it.

Give your prospect time to feel your product or service. Let them hear the sounds of your incredible offer. Let them see the luxury that is before them. Let them feel that softness that only comes ever so often. Let them taste the concept in their mouths. Let them bond with it as if it was theirs from the very beginning. Let them feel as if you have something they want, or that is actually theirs already.

Turn your prospect's lack of need into a want just because they'd love to have it. Make them imagine the many things they can do with your offer. Build their ego up with the stature of having something that not everyone has the privilege to own.

Speak in the future tense so they may imagine purchasing something that they have not yet. Use the phrase "When you…" as in, "When you put this next to your aquarium at home, you will see how great they blend together."

Tell your prospect that your product or service fits them, as a wedding dress on a bride-to-be. Allow them to unite the product or service into their imagination, like two halves joining as one. (This relationship was meant to be.) They and your service are one.

Ask your prospect, "How does it feel?" "How does it taste?" "How does it look?" "How does it sound?" "How does it smell?" Get all their senses involved, and let them use their own lips to seal the deal by saying, "It feels good!" Then say, "Good." Then be silent and change the subject.

Tell your prospect to look into the future, and "What do you see?" "Do you see yourself waking up next Tuesday morning with this new, lovely car in your garage?" "Or do you see yourself waking up inside the car in your garage?" Use humor to stimulate their mind about the reality of taking home your service or product, leaving you behind, all alone, with nothing but a smile.

# Topic 61

---

## YOUR URGENCY IS WHAT WILL COMPEL THEM TO ACT NOW

*What may be done at any time will be done at no time.*
*- Scottish proverb*

You have to make the prospect know that now is the time to act, or else they will become lackadaisical about time. You have to show and convince them about the urgency of now. You have to let them know that you are a busy person, and that your service or product is busy as well. You cannot give them the impression that they can have it anytime they wish, or for the same price they currently see. You have to let them know that the price is right and the time is right now. "Now is the best time to claim this product because we are offering some special discounts to valued customers like yourself, TODAY." The price may just go up in a few days, so you must let them know that now is the time to catch the fish, while they are abundant, rather than when there is a scarcity. Why? For when there is a scarcity of product or service, then prices go up. That is the basics of any class in marketing.

You want to come across to your prospect as if you will never be able to see them again if they don't act now. You want to send off the message that things will never be the same again if they don't act now. You want to treat it as a matter of life or a life long lost if your prospect does not register with you right now. You want to show your prospect the eclipse that is happening now, and not to wait a year or perhaps even a lifetime before seeing it again. You want to let the prospect know that if they don't act now it is almost like throwing a valuable diamond into the sea, for no apparent reason. You want to let the prospect know that your offer comes about only three times in an entire lifetime.

190

You want to rush the prospect into acting now, before the bulls in Spain come rushing down the street after them. You want them to "hurry, hurry, hurry" before the category 5 hurricane hits town. You want your prospect to move quickly before the tsunami wave comes rushing up upon the doorstep to their house. You want to let them know that you are serious about them acting now, or else they will miss this opportunity forever.

You want to let the prospect know that you are not leaving until they give you a definite yes or no to your offer. You want to let the prospect know that the fact that they will have to think about it is giving you a big headache. You want to let them know the fact that they will have to get back to you is making your back hurt. You want to let them know the fact that they will have to speak to someone else before making a decision is giving you a sore throat. You want to let them know the fact that they will have to shop around is making you feel cheaper than the product you are trying to sell them. You want to let them know the fact that they will give you a call when they're ready is hurting your eardrums; and that's not what you want to hear. You want to let your prospect know the fact that they can't afford it is not a good enough reason to not claim the offer. "Sure you can afford it. If you expected me to believe that, you wouldn't have said that, right?"

Fear walking away from the sale more than standing up against the face of opposition. Fear the thought of turning your back empty handed more than your annoying presence still in front of the prospect. Fear the idea of them selling you the idea that they are not ready to buy more than your desire to give it to them right here and now. Fear the notion of them doing a better job at selling than you can as an embarrassment to your profession. Create the urgency that will make it next to impossible, if not uncomfortable, for them to want to refuse you and your offer.

The bottom line to your presentation is to emphasize the word "now" or "today," and not another day because you are busy. Look the prospect STRAIGHT in the eyes to create tension, and tell them straight out, "Take this home today." Be firm, and don't look away because if your prospect sees any hesitation or uncertainty within you, then they will use that as an escape route to make another excuse not to claim your offer today. "Now" and "today" are the key words to your urgency.

If all else fails, then make them an offer they can't refuse: Tell the prospect that you will allow them to take your product or service now, and if they still don't like it, then you'll take it back, AT NO CHARGE. "Sounds fair?" Of course it does. And if even this fails, then set up an appointment for a later time.

# Topic 62

## DO NOT TALK TO YOUR PROSPECTS – ENGAGE THEM IN CONVERSATION

*Conversation is the fine art of mutual consideration and communication about matters of common interest that basically have some human importance.*
  *- Ordway Tead*

Do not talk *to* your prospect – talk *with* them. Invite them to have a conversation with you. For a conversation is the raw material needed to make a sale. Turn the words "sales presentation" into the word "conversation" if you really intend to enjoy the method of selling as a career in which you can feel comfortable being in.

Talk with your prospect about what they like. Talk with them about what they dislike. Talk with them about life. Talk with them about themselves. Talk with them about who you are. Talk with them about why you want to use your profession to build a relationship with them. Talk with them about their family. Talk with them about what makes them happy. Talk with them like a real person. Even though Sales involves a lot of numbers and statistics, do not look at any of your prospects as a number or a statistic – look at them as a part of your family tree.

Prospects hate the idea of buying something they were sold – but ironically, they love the idea of buying what they decided they should buy. Don't make them feel as if they are being sold, make them know that they sold themselves into buying – make them see that they sold themselves into buying. Convince them that they are making an educated decision. Boost up their ego by letting them know they made or are making a good choice.

Don't have debates with your prospects, have conversations with them. Do not make presentations to them; discuss issues with them like a real

193

person. Make them feel comfortable with someone, namely you, who is comfortable to speak with.

Engage your prospects into listening to what you have to say because what you have to say will benefit them. Make them want to listen to what you have to say because what you have to say is all about them. Make them take what you say to heart because what you have to say is good for them.

Find out what your prospect likes and grab hold of it. Keep their interest high by holding a conversation that involves all the things they like. Keep the conversation going by emphasizing your interest in providing or wanting to give them what they like. Don't stop talking until they are convinced that you have what they like. Then give them what they want and like. Talk about nothing other than what they like.

Involve yourself in the life of your prospect. Show them how you and what you have to offer them will fit into their life. Let them know that they have room for you in their life; and that you are in fact already a part of their life. Don't stop speaking until you've convinced them that the relationship between both of you, and what you have to offer them were meant to be.

Find even more common ground to talk about. Switch the conversation again if need be from your product or service, or from negotiating price, to what fine restaurant they visited two weeks ago with some other companion of theirs. Ask them about *the when, the how, the who* and *the what* that went on in that fine restaurant that you too want to visit in the near future. Encourage them to talk about the fine wine and medium rare steak they enjoyed so very much. All this must be making you hungry also. Do not talk to your prospects, talk with them and engage them in conversation; and they will want to listen and be more involved with you and your message.

# Topic 63

## IT'S NOT WHAT YOU SAY, BUT HOW YOU SAY IT THAT WILL MAKE THE DIFFERENCE

*People don't ask for facts in making up their minds. They would rather have one good, soul-satisfying emotion than a dozen facts.*
*- Robert Keith Leavitt*

The act of persuasion mostly involves speaking from your heart and not your head. If persuasion involved using mostly logic, then we would all be sharing the same opinions about everything. Persuasion is making others feel and connect to your passion, and act upon it. The most reliable way to convince someone to listen to you is not with your intellect, but with your passion.

Passion is the feeling that comes from deep within your soul. Passion is the ocean of your stomach forcing waves of enthusiasm from your mouth. Passion is the fire within you that never burns out. Passion is a powerful conviction that yearns to explode (like a volcanic eruption!)

When you speak to your prospects, do not speak from the mouth or the head. Instead, speak from the gut and the heart. Summon up your most powerful of feelings to express your most wonderful of thoughts. Overcome the prospect's objections with your conviction, so that they will gasp with amazement.

Speak with feelings and not with words. Utter with conviction and not with sounds. Make them feel your passion.

If you are speaking with a prospect on the phone, then smile slightly, so that they may sense the pleasant look upon your face. Speak slowly and thoughtfully. (They shall not interrupt you.) Feel yourself being in control.

Anyone who speaks with passion is going to be speaking with enthusiasm. Anyone who speaks with zeal is going to be speaking with emphasis. Highlight the words that you want your prospect to pay specially attention to. Pause after making valid statements, so that they can absorb your jewels of wisdom. Speak assuredly so that they'll know you're there for them.

Speak with a strong belief and a deep conviction in what you're saying. Compel them to swim in the waters of your passion.

Shake the earth with the sounds of your voice. Move the clouds with the words you use. Summon the wind with the enthusiasm you bring. Make it rain with the empathy you share.

The more passionate you are, the more successful you will be in sales. Passion is only a song and dance. If you can't sing well, then hum softly. If you can't dance well, then clap your hands and tap your feet. Be creative and innovative, and where you are lacking, make up for it by substituting other resources that are available. Be inventive. Don't give in if you don't have a match to light the flames of your passion. Use the little spark available to make fire from the woods of your desire. (That little that you have is enough to cause a forest fire.)

Speak with understanding and compassion with those who need it. Interrupt your routine to accommodate the emotional state of others. Speak softly so they can hear you loudly. Hug them with your words. Embrace them with your feelings of compassion.

Make the prospect feel the thunder of your zeal, even if your words are nothing but whispers. Make them feel your presence and see your enthusiasm for the product or service you know they will claim.

# Topic 64

---

## HOW TO KEEP PROSPECTS SAYING "YES"

*We cannot direct the wind, but we can adjust the sails.*
*- Anonymous*

This is NOT the typical 'yes set' theory whereby a salesperson asks a prospect a bunch of questions such as, "Is this your name?" or "Do you live at this location?" with the intent that the prospect will continue the pattern of saying yes when it comes time to close the sale. A lot of prospects have picked up on this form of selling and have become immune, as well as annoyed with it.

This alternative form of getting prospects to say "yes" is more sophisticated and is so effective that you will wonder why you didn't consider it more often, even though you may have probably heard it or used it yourself many times before.

Start by stating something as if it is factual, and confirm it as being fact by asking a question that confirms it. This is known as a "tie-down" or tag question. The purpose of a tag question is to impose your idea or belief as if it was factual, and then by almost telling the prospect to agree with you, in the form of a question.

✓ You want to be happy, right?

✓ You like to buy good products, true?

✓ You can afford that, can't you?

✓ To be fair, you should first take a look at it before you come to a conclusion, shouldn't you?

✓ That's fair, isn't it?

✓ You love that, don't you?

✓ You want the best for less, isn't that so?

✓ You like this item – correct?

✓ That's great, right?

✓ Amazing, isn't it?

✓ It's easy, right?

Tag questions are really great and easy to use. They put you in a position of control, which is exactly where you want to be. They also keep the prospect under control because the prospect does not want to say no to something that seems obviously true.

A tag question lowers the prospect's defenses by not *telling* them to say "yes," but by *asking* them to say yes. It is a subtle form of command to agree with you, or otherwise seem out of place. If done correctly the prospect will feel uncomfortable saying "no" to a tag question that they should be saying "*yes*" to.

Tag questions give you an edge because you can create a large number of them and get the prospect to say "yes" to each one. Getting the prospect in the rhythm of saying "yes" will give you an advantage when they say "*yes*" to your final request at the end. When you have managed to get the prospect into a pattern or habit of saying "yes," they will feel awkward breaking this rhythm. Tag questions forces prospects to maintain a *yes* mentality.

You can try tag questions not only in selling items and services, but also as a general form of communication when you desire people to agree with you. You may use it on dates, in general conversation and in debates. They can even be used on yourself to convince yourself of an idea.

Your body language should also match the tag questions you're using with your prospects.

*Raise your eyebrows, open your eyes wide and nod your head when you are asking such questions. This will create the correct coordination that is needed to convince the prospect to agree with this method of questioning.*

You do not want to use this method to an obvious extent with a prospect, or else they may pick up on it and get annoyed. And you will have lost the effect and purpose of what you were trying to accomplish. So be somewhat subtle in this approach. Use it moderately and sparingly when deemed beneficial, if you want it to produce the desired effect. Using it fifteen times in half an hour would be great; but I've heard it said and have seen it written that if you can get a prospect to say *"yes"* forty-five times in forty-five minutes, then you've automatically completed a sale. (Great topic, *right?*)

# Topic 65

---

## LET YOUR CUSTOMERS BRING YOU MORE CUSTOMERS

*If you do build a great experience, customers tell each other about that. Word of mouth is very powerful.*
      *- Jay Abraham*

You will develop life long customers if you treat them the way a customer expects to be treated. They will be loyal to you if you are honest and true with them. They will not forsake you if you remain true to your promises.

They will recommend their friends to you if you ask them to. And to their friends will they recommend you if you request them to. Some of them will even recommend you without your need to ask. But to be on the safe, always ask.

Don't be afraid to tell your customers to, "Go forth, and multiply the earth." Don't hesitate to let them know that you need more wonderful customers like them.

You must think in the business sense if you plan to be employed in Sales as a career. A good businessperson knows the key to success: duplication. The only way you are going to duplicate your customer base is by asking your current and satisfied customers to bring you more customers. Studies show that it is five times easier to generate new customers from your existing customers than to get new customers on your own.

Some salespeople thrive with the referrals they receive year after year from their former satisfied customers. They were wise enough to foresee a future when they would need to use their own customers to work for them.

Open up the business of referrals by asking your satisfied customers to provide the capital for you. Use each and every one of your customers as a source of advertisement to get more customers. Let your customers do wonders for you. And they will, not from a sense of being forced, but by an inner urge that compels them to do something good back to someone who has been good to them.

Treat your customers with respect and they will pay you back with their respect. They will not hesitate to assist you in your business of customer-based referrals. It will not come as work to them, but as joy; like friends helping friends. It will not be a burden to them, but a natural instinct. It will become a part of their pastime chitchats that their own friends and families must go and see this wonderful salesperson who taught them all things they never knew.

A serious salesperson is going to have two main things, no three – a book of notes, a pen and a list of customer referrals. Check off your newest referral with a pen in that notebook of yours.

Customers are lost everyday from a lack of asking. Simply ask, and an abundance of customers you shall receive. Don't feel shy or ashamed, but be bold and strong with your head up and a smile on your face.

Your referral customers are the easiest customers to satisfy because they have already been satisfied with the good things they've heard about you. The sale becomes a 1-2-3 step instead of a back and forth dance that goes nowhere.

So let your customers bring you more customers, so you may bring them more service, so you can bring yourself more money into your bank account with less effort, so your business may thrive. You become an official and professional salesman or saleswoman when you engage in the businessman's or businesswoman's way of doing real business. Sales is not sales. Sales is business. And business is the domino effect of people everywhere referring other people to you and your business wherever. Turn your satisfied customers into personal ambassadors – proclaiming to everyone of your good deeds.

# Topic 66

---

## DON'T TELL THEM THE PRICE – SHOW THEM THE PRICE

*In business, you don't get what you deserve, you get what you negotiate.*
   *- Chester L. Karrass*

Getting the prospect all fired up about your product and ready to buy is only half the battle. The next half involves telling them the price. But in this case you will not be telling them the price, you will be showing them the price. This will take half the burden off your shoulders. They will see for themselves what the price is, and you won't even have to say a word. After all, seeing is believing! This will add legitimacy to the price for the mere fact that they will be seeing it for themselves with their own eyes, rather than hearing it from the tentative sound of your voice.

After completing the presentation and demonstrations, the final step before the close is to let the prospect know how much they are going to spend for their product or service. When this time comes, simply write, type or show a printed version of the final numbers on your working paper, or on the *agreement*, then show it to the prospect and say, "This is what you'll pay." Say it with a firm voice.

Some prospects will ask you what the price is before its time. And you will handle this by letting the prospect know that they must not disturb the hen from laying before its time, or else all they will have are premature eggs. If the prospect asks what the price is before you get a chance to show them how they will benefit from your product, you may say, "I'll get to that in a minute. But I just want to show you this first." If they insist, then you have to remind the prospect of an earlier statement you had made to them. What is that earlier statement, you may ask?

Before showing any prospect your product or service, be sure to cover how you will handle price before they bring it up. *Let the prospect know, in the most diplomatic manner possible, that you are going to show them all the fine features and benefits of your product or service, and then share the price with them afterwards.* You may give them a general idea by saying something like:

- ✓ "I understand you need the price; and I'll give you all the information, including taxes and everything else. Just let me show you what I have first, okay?"
- ✓ "We'll give you the best price possible. Don't worry. Let me show you what I have."
- ✓ "It's going to work out cheaper on a quality basis than your current product/service"
- ✓ "The price is going to range anywhere from two to four dollars per day, depending on which one(s) you choose. Let's see which one(s) you like."
- ✓ "The price depends on which service you choose. Let's pick out the things you like and I'll add it all up for you."
- ✓ "The price you see is negotiable. Let's see if you like it and then we'll discuss the numbers. Fair enough?"

Give these general statements beforehand so that when it comes time for the prospect to *harass* you about price, you will be able to remind them about your earlier promise.

So, if a prospect asks you what the price is during the process of demonstrating the benefits to them, simply say something like, "Remember what I promised you earlier? You will be paying less than what you're paying currently for your service! I'll show you the price in just a little while."

When you are sharing the price of your product or service with the prospect, be sure to write the numbers very large and boldly. Wimpy, skimpy handwriting with small numbers will not impress the prospect very much. But the larger and more intimidating the numbers are, the more the prospect will feel compelled to go along with it. Why? The larger the writing, the more legitimacy it carries within the prospect's subconscious mind. It tells them you have nothing to hide and that you are proud of your product or service to the point whereby you know your price offer is fair, and you're not afraid to show it to anyone.

## Rules on price:

When presenting a price to the prospect, if you can, always make sure you leave enough room to discount the price three times. Why? Prospects are always looking for discounts no matter how low your initial offer is. That is the nature of sales. If your product or service does not offer discounts then always present the most expensive product or service to the prospect first. If they can't afford it then show them a cheaper item. If they still can't afford it then show them the next cheapest item available. Studies show that if a prospect is presented with three items and cannot afford the most expensive product or service they're presented with first, then they'll be more inclined to buy the *middle item*.

## Tips on price presentation:

When you're showing the price to a prospect you want to be extra enthusiastic that second or so just *before* showing it to them. You may want to add a statement like this: "Remember when I promised you earlier that you will only be paying between $2 and $4 a day, well here it is." Then show them the price of **$83.97** per month. "That works out to less than $3 per day." (You kept your promise.) If the purchase price is thousands of dollars, you may also try saying something like, "I have some good news for you. You will *only* be paying this much per month. Then show them the price, for example, of: **$351.91**.

Avoid even numbers. Odd numbers are harder for prospects to calculate in their heads.

## Important tips on presenting price:

Just before showing a prospect the price, you should be hyper, excited and enthusiastic. But as soon as they see the price, you're demeanor should change immediately. You should suddenly become serious and quiet. Why? You mean business! All smiles end for you until the prospect agrees with the price.

After showing the prospect the price, *say nothing. He who speaks first loses.* Even if the prospect looks at the price for twenty minutes without saying a word, you too must be silent. You must not utter a word. All along, you must be looking straight *between* the eyes of the prospect while they are looking at the price. You should be looking between their eyes because it makes them feel more uncomfortable than looking into their eyes, and that is what you want during this particular process. Do not take your eyes off them, and do not say a word, or else you will lose. Why? You want to build up tension and trust so the prospect will feel a need to end the tension and trust you. Let the prospect end the tension. Don't let it be you or else you'll lose.

After the prospect agrees to the price then you can relax and start smiling again. If the prospect wants to negotiate the price, and you are able to do so, then let them know you will find out if you can do it. Get a firm commitment from the prospect by using the if/will close: "I'll have to speak with my manager, Susan, but *if* my manager can reduce this by $10 off, *will* you take this sofa home today?"

If the prospect totally disagrees with the price and wants to leave, you may voluntarily agree to give them a discount. If that doesn't work then give them a second discount. If that still doesn't work then give them a third and final discount.

Your discounts should not have big gaps. They should follow in a sequence of logical and lower amounts, like $30 off, then another $20 off, then another $10 off. Do not create an irregular sequence of discounts, like $90 off, then $55 off, then $150 off. Your discounts should lessen each time you offer one.

*Unless the prospect is paying cash in full, try not to sell price; instead, sell monthly payments to your prospects.* The price of the product or service "does not really matter" if they are agreeing to make monthly payments. Try to steer them away from price, and lead them to the final monthly payment. This will help you keep the original price without discounting it, and ultimately put more money into your pocket and less stress on your table, as a salesperson.

# Topic 67

## A CLOSER LOOK AT NEGOTIATING PRICE

*Show me a good and gracious loser, and I'll show you a failure.*
        *- Knute Rockne*

Before negotiating price with any prospective buyer, there are three main prerequisites that you must abide by:

1. Make sure you have built rapport with the prospect. See Topic10, *How To Build Rapport For Sure.*
2. Make sure you have chosen a product or service in the price range that the prospect can possibly afford.
3. Make sure you settle on a product or service that the prospect likes. Ask them the from 1 to 10 question: "From a scale of 1 to 10 – 10 being the best – how do you like this X?"

The reason why you want to build rapport with a prospect is so that they will not give you a hard time during the negotiation process. If a prospect wants to give you a hard time during the negotiating process, then that could be an indication that you did not, or were not able to, build rapport with them.

The only way to know if a prospect can afford your product or service is by doing some investigating into the prospect's financial situation. You can do so by asking them what price range they were looking for before showing them anything. Then you can figure out which product or service fits the prospect's budget. You may want to find out if the prospect even has a job, by asking them the *rapport-building question,* "So, what do you do for a living?"

When a prospect does not like your product or service, that is all the more reason why they will give you a hard time during the bargaining

206

process. People don't like to bargain too much for what they like – their love for it will make them willing to pay the extra money. Be sure the prospect likes the product or service before negotiating price.

Present your price to the prospect with a *highball* offer, meaning a price that starts out high; and that can be lowered. You must do this to create room for the prospect who wants to feel that they have accomplished something by not agreeing with your first offer. Remember, you – as a salesperson – can always go down in price, but never up.

If a prospect gives you a lowball offer – which is completely outside the possibility of making a profit – it is time to use your negotiating skills. For instance, if you make an offer to a prospect of $18,999, and they counter-offer with $14,000, then handle them like this:

***First***, look visibly surprised at their *ridiculous* offer.

***Second***, immediately tell them you can't accept their offer.
Follow up by using some or all these suggestions:

- ✓ That's too low.
- ✓ *We want to earn your business!* (This compliment is important. It will make them less resistant towards you.)
- ✓ There is not a lot of mark-up in our cost. The price is already discounted.
- ✓ Our cost for the product/service is more than that – $14,000.
- ✓ Where did you get that number from?
- ✓ (If the prospect says someone else told them it would be a good offer, then ask them, "Where did your friend get that number from?")
- ✓ Do you like the product or service? (If they say, "yes," then ask them: "Then why are you devaluing it what that low offer?")
- ✓ If it was up to me, I would give it to you for that price, but I can't.
- ✓ I hope you understand that we need to make a little profit.

✓ (If the prospect is paying by monthly payments, then switch from price, to monthly payments.) "What monthly payments were you looking for – around $350 for 60 months? Payments are more important for you than price, right?"

✓ There's not much I can do about the price, but I can loosen up the monthly payments a little bit.

✓ (Depending on the relationship between you and the prospect, try to kid around with them.) "Why are you giving me a hard time? Don't you like me anymore?"

✓ I know you don't want the hassle of negotiating price. I know you want the product/service for a reasonable price, right? This is a good price.

✓ Help me.

✓ The reason why the price may seem high is because that product/service holds its value.

✓ I know that $18,999 is a lot of money, but you're getting a really fair/good deal.

✓ That product/service has your name on it, and it wants you to take it home today, without the two of us fighting over it. You'll look good with it.

✓ I'll be proud to have you as a new customer.

✓ Besides price, is there something else that is preventing you from taking this order today?

✓ (If at all possible, show the prospect supporting data that suggests that your price offer is fair.)

*Third*, step by step, go through the features and demonstrate the benefits your product or service offers that justifies its cost. Build value, like a building made out of gold.

*Fourth*, ask the prospect to give you a new and reasonable offer that comes as close as possible to your offer of $18,999.

**Fifth**, if the prospect does not want to come close to your original offer, tell them that you will split the difference with them. Come half way between your offer, and theirs: $16,999. Let the prospect know that you may not be able to do it, but you'll try. Then ask them, "If I can get you this for $16,999, will you take the product/service home today?" If they say "yes," then remove yourself from the situation, and go *see* if you can accommodate their offer. If they still want to haggle, then stand firm. Don't let them intimidate you. Have a thick skin. Break off the point of negotiation, and let them know that this is your final offer. "My well is dry. I can't lower this any further."

**Sixth**, see if you can switch the product or service to a lower priced product or service – "I have something less expensive to show you" – or if you can extend the monthly terms, from say 60 months to 72 months, then recommend it to your prospect.

**Seventh**, maintain eye contact at least 98% of the time during the negotiation process. This will increase your chance of getting an agreement out of the prospect. Eye contact indicates confidence is within you, and builds trust from within the prospect's perception of you.

**Eighth**, be calm during the whole negotiation process. Don't lose control. For instance, if the prospect gets up and says, "I'm leaving," you must remain seated. You do not want to show any signs of desperation or being intimidated by the prospect. Look them straight in the eye, and convince them with your stare.

❖

Negotiating is easiest when there is good rapport between you and the prospect, and especially when they are presented with a product or service that is affordable to them. Don't sabotage your effort by skipping even one of these vital steps.

# Topic 68

## DON'T GIVE 'EM TIME TO THINK

*The present moment is creative, creating with an unheard-of intensity.*
  *- Le Corbusier*

This topic deals with a method that many sales professionals have "discovered" and use with amazing effectiveness to increase their sales output.

When dealing with a prospect, always keep at the back of your mind that you have about two minutes to make the prospect decide that "yes," they are going to claim your offer. In order to do this, you must be quick in your strategy to do a preview of your service or product, emphasizing the features, and *especially* the benefits within that two-minute period, so the prospect will be overcome with thoughts of anxiousness. Using different arguments or reasons, your aim is to impress upon the prospect why they should claim your offer right away, so they won't have time to really think about it logically. You have to appeal to their emotion, which is weaker than their logic.

The two-minute preview will set the stage for whether or not the prospect is going to claim your offer and how soon. Your aim is to sum up all the main reasons why the prospect should claim your offer within that two-minute span, so as to leave an impression upon their emotions. The goal is to overcome them to the point whereby they cannot think or rationalize your offer, other than to just agree with what you're saying. You'll do the thinking for them. You'll be the assurance to them of what is best for them because you are the physician, and they are your patient.

After the two-minute preview you may relax a little – but only a little. If you believe you've made an impact on their emotions to claim your offer without rationalizing what just happened, then you have done your job.

Remember, they did not know you were coming for them, but you knew you were just waiting for them. You are the professional and they are the novice. You are the lion and they are the deer caught in the headlights. You are the boss and they are the boss' favorite "target."

Be quick and rush through your offer for the first two minutes. Hurry through the process strategically so they will not know what just hit them. Make them say "yes" without knowing what they are saying "yes" to. Speed up the velocity of your words, so they do not hear or understand you. Overcome them 'til they grow weary.

Don't give 'em time to think or else you lose and they win. The moment the prospect gets a grip of the situation and a hand on the handlebar, you lose. You must consider Sales as a profession that is *very* time sensitive. A lot of selling involves timing. And the timing must be right and quick if it is to be effective. Just like a joke's punch line must be timed correctly, so too must certain sensitive strategies be implemented to make the sale effective and potent.

Just like an open bottle of carbonated cola must be consumed within a certain period of time before it loses its fizz, so too must certain aspects in Sales be implemented before they become flat, ineffective and tasteless.

Be fully prepared for your prospect or else they will be fully prepared for you the moment they catch you off guard.

A thoughtful prospect is a dangerous prospect because a thoughtful prospect will protect their emotions from buying from you. And since most sales are made on an emotional basis that will defeat the point you are trying to create. Therefore, you must be quick to stir up the prospect emotionally, and to create within them a craving to want what you have rather than thinking about if they need it.

A volcanic eruption happens suddenly, and so should you be quick to collect the larva of your prospect's emotions. Build up the intensity. Make them want it. And make them want it now. Don't give them time to think. Get them to act now, and ask questions later.

You are a great salesperson when, after completing a sale, the prospect says to themselves, "Now what just happened?" "Did we just buy something here?" But don't worry, as you're walking away from your new sale and new found customer; they will chuckle and say how good you are at what you do – you were really good. And guess what – they'll still love you.

# Topic 69

## INSPIRE THEM BY WHAT THEY FEAR

*Football games aren't won, they're lost.*
*- Fielding Yost*

In sales, there is something in particular the prospect fears most. They are most concerned about the fear of loss or not having. In fact, studies have shown that people are more concerned about losing what they have more so than gaining what they don't have. This may sound disappointing to the salesperson whose mindset is to present their product or service as a gain to the prospect rather than preventing the loss of something. How then can you tailor your presentation as the fear of loss, versus the desire to gain?

Instead of suggesting to your prospect that they will gain and be saving money by switching to your service, show them how they are losing money right now by not having your service. Instead of just demonstrating the comforts and reliability they will gain with your service, emphasize the danger and risk they are taking by not having your service. Your product or service fulfills a desire or a need that fulfills a void within the prospect. This is what you want your prospect to believe and know and see.

In order to inspire your prospect you must churn up their desire to want what you have. You must inspire their inner urge to feel a sense of need for what you have. You must show them that they are naked without your offer; and they are in need of clothing. You must show them that your product is a necessity, just as their sense of taste is necessary. They need it not for the sake of gaining something but for the fear of losing something.

Sound the alarm! Give the prospect three good reasons why your offer is necessary for them to take now.

**Reason #1**: They will not have to worry about losing sleep as long as they have your service. Your service provides peace of mind to your prospect that they are not receiving now. They will have a back up just in case something goes wrong.

**Reason #2:** They will not be losing the large amount of time they are losing now. Your service makes things quicker and more efficient for them. Your service is fast and convenient.

**Reason #3:** They will not be losing the vitality and good health they are otherwise losing now by not having your service. Your service provides a healthy environment and ultimately fewer visits to the doctor in the future. Remember here, prevention is always better than a cure.

## Provide them with this true philosophy:
Safety, reliability and comfort are number one. It is not what they can see that they should be concerned about; it is what they cannot see. Prepare them for the possibility of losing out in the future.

Inspire your prospect by the fear of *what if* something undesirable happens if they don't act now. "What if the price goes up when you really need it?" "What if you can't get it when you really need it?"

The key to remembering this technique is to always be aware that there is something for the prospect to *lose* if they don't gain your product or service now.

Your product or service will provide peace of mind for the prospect the day they find themselves in dire need or want.

Keep your ground. Don't back down, but give good reasons as a backup why they should claim your product or service now, and not later. Your product was not made because people don't need it. Your product or service was made because necessity is the mother of invention. There is a reason why your company is in business.

*Whisper with a soft voice.* Inspire them with your plea. Utilize the power word "please."

Provoke them into action by their fears. Provide them with the answer to a question that has not yet been asked. Be the umbrella in the trunk of their car on a sudden rainy day. Be the security alarm that sounds when the thief comes in the night. Give them the peace of mind of knowing a vehicle with side airbags is the wisest choice against that crazy driver aiming towards them carelessly. Let your offer be their peace of mind that secures them firmly from the front, back, sides, top and bottom. Bolt them securely with your offer and plea.

# Topic 70

## MAKE THEM AN OFFER THEY CAN'T REFUSE

*Beauty itself doth of itself persuade The eyes of man without an orator.*
  *- William Shakespeare*

One of the basics of selling yourself to anyone is to make them an offer that appeals to them. Everyday, millions of people who know nothing about the professional method of selling use the method of, "If you do this for me, then I will do this for you." For example, "If you lend me $20, then I will give you back $40 in one week." This is referred to as the "If you X, then I will X" offer.

Tell your prospect, "If you give me 5 minutes of your time, then I will show you how to save up to $500." Present an offer to them that whets their appetite. Spark their curiosity by making them want to learn more. Make them desire to know, "How are you going to go through with your offer?" Or make them wonder, "Are you really going to go through with that offer?" Make them feel the fairness and benefits of your offer – something they won't want to refuse.

And furthermore, you want to make a special promise to your prospect that will entice them. You want them to know that there is something beneficial for them by agreeing to your offer. You want them to feel and know that your deal is a fair deal that should not be refused.

Present to the prospect a tantalizing offer that will make their mouth water. Make them want to test your ability to fulfill the promise. Give them three for the price of one. But all they have to do is to give you one chance first. Tell them that if they give you an hour of their time, then you will show them two-thirds of the kingdom of Egypt. Beseech them that if they buy your product you will give them one month *free* of charge.

216

Let them know that if they give you a glass of water you will reduce their bill by $1,000, every year.

Be enticing. Show them a little and make them beg for more. Tease their curiosity to the point that they must follow you. Flirt with their minds to make them want to spend an hour with you.

Make your offer a very attractive one. Decorate it with bows and red ribbons. Present it to them in a rounded box. Give it to them with a thank you note attached.

Prospects do not eat with their mouths. Prospect eat with their eyes. The offer must look appealing, or else they won't eat it, even if the taste is very good.

Speak with feeling and not with words. Express yourself from the heart and not the mind, if you intend to gain the prospect's interest. Dig deep inside of yourself until you find a ruby to show unto the prospect. Put it before their eyes so that it may glitter like the sunset. Create a sense of wonder and amazement. Make them relish coming into your world. Create a pathway within their minds that they will not want to leave. Enchant them with your charm and wit.

Prospects are not blown away by what you say and by what they hear, but by the image that you have created within their minds. Speak with colorful words. Use images that they can remember. Use words that are sweet to listen to. Make music in their eardrums. Create a sound that will make them dance. Whisper a tune that will make them melt.

Present to them an offer that they can't refuse: "Joan, I want you to be completely honest with me. If I can give you the best service that you *deserve*, at the best price you're *entitled* to, tell me that you'll take it today. If I can't do as I propose, tell me that I didn't do my job. Agreed?" "Are you sure?" "Positive?" "Great!"

# Topic 71

---

## CONVINCE THEM BY THEIR OWN WORDS

*People are usually more convinced by reasons they discovered themselves than by those found out by others.*
        *- Blaise Pascal*

It is true that people like to convince themselves of things rather than have someone else convince them. For seemingly good reasons we reckon our own thoughts as the final judgment as to what's best for us. This is an interesting observation. For with such an observation, a salesperson can use a person's own thoughts to convince them of a fact or a situation. How?

The only way you are going to know what a person likes is to ask them questions. We are not meant to be mind readers. As long as a prospect truly tells you what he or she likes, especially about your product or service, then you can use what they say back to them as a reference. In doing so, you will be pointing out to them that it is not your thought, but theirs.

For example, if a prospect says they like peach roses, and you are the owner of a flower shop, then your natural instinct would be to sell them what you have. If they were to later object by saying that they will have to think about it before purchasing, your comeback would be, "You like peach roses, right?" And they would naturally say "yes." Your response could then be, "Well I have all the peach roses you need. I'll even water them for you. Remember what you said, 'You like peach roses!' I'm only here to give you what you want. Take the peach roses today, and I'll give you an extra 5 percent off. Is there something else besides peach roses that you'd like?"

Always go back to what a prospect said when they are showing forgetfulness. Always remind them that it is not you who said it; that they

218

are the ones who like "peach roses." You are not forcing them to take something they don't like. Your job is only to give them what they want without them wasting time, or ending up choosing something later on they don't like. Their first instinct is the best instinct.

This is why it is so important to know what the prospect is thinking and what they like. If you don't know what they like then you won't know what to sell them. But if you ask and they tell you what turns them on, then your job is to turn them on some more by giving them exactly what they want.

*Accuse* your prospect of their lack of loyalty towards themselves. Were they lying when they said they liked peach roses? If not, then what's the problem? "Here are the peach roses at a discounted price, but only for today."

Prospects don't usually like to go against what they say – it makes them feel awkward and silly in their own eyes. That's why it is a very important part of our jobs as salespeople to keep an open ear towards our prospects. Listen so you may be able to testify later against the prospect who is not true to his or her word. Convince them that they know what's best for them because they said so. Show them that it doesn't make sense for them to deny themselves what they like best. Let them see that their first instinct is always the best.

Let the prospect rationalize what you say about what they've said. It will all come back to them that they were the one who said it. And they won't disagree with themselves. And guess what? They know what's best for themselves. (It all came from the horse's mouth.) "Peach roses." They cannot go against themselves because they are in harmony with themselves. They are not obligated to you or anyone else, but surely, to their own selves be true.

# Topic 72

## WHAT GOES ON IN THE MIND OF A SUCCESSFUL SALESPERSON

*Success usually comes to those who are too busy to be looking for it.*
*- Henry David Thoreau*

A successful salesperson first believes in his or her self. They have conquered the voice of doubt that tells them they won't achieve. They have overcome their toughest customer – their own self. They have envisioned success before it happened. It's not a matter of if they will succeed, but how soon.

The successful salesperson finds a way to like what they do. They look forward to the opportunity of turning prospects into loyal customers. Life is not a bed of roses, and so they have made up their minds to create their own beds of roses.

A successful salesperson plans to empathize with their prospects. They know that a successful relationship involves putting their feet into others' shoes. They know just how to put prospects at ease. They feel what they feel, and see what they see; and understand what they think. Their feet grow weary from walking in many shoes.

The successful salesperson has a business mentality. She keeps a pen and notebook handy, taking notes and names of referrals that she asks for from her customers. This lady is a business woman, for sure.

A successful salesperson knows that they must show enthusiasm and passion for their product or service if they intend to persuade others to do the same. Their eyes are wide awake, and their hands are dancing with excitement. They are like a breath of fresh air. They are like excited horses galloping in a field. (The field of life is a colorful place indeed.)

The successful salesperson knows that in order to be successful with anything, one must consistently be persistent. One or two attempts at doing something is not enough in the mind of a salesperson who wants to win. Persistency is a major weapon in winning the battle of the prospect's objections. (May the best soul win!)

A successful salesperson takes rejections and objections as they come. They never take such things personally. They always look at things as they happen, instead of things happening to them. You will never see a successful salesperson walking away with their tail between their legs.

The successful salesperson is focused because one slight distraction can cause a domino effect, leading to all sorts of distractions. "Do not disturb," is the sign the successful salesperson carries on his forehead. A successful salesperson is in control of themselves and the situations around them. He does not wait for things to happen – he makes things happen. "Action Jackson" is his name. And *machine in motion* is what they know him by.

The successful salesperson has a stronger willpower than that of the prospect. For every reason the prospect has not to buy, that salesperson has an extra reason why to buy. The battle between David and Goliath begins. And there is that successful salesperson, in between, cheering them on.

A successful salesperson knows that changing minds is all about changing opinions. And in that successful salesperson's opinion, opinions are weak, like pigeons are smelly. They do not mind friendly challenges to take a prospect head on, wit for wit. (Trophies aren't for losers.)

The successful salesperson knows that they do not need to depend on luck if they already have positive thinking as their halo. The choice of looking at the bright side of life is all the good luck they will ever need to succeed. A light shines upon them – a ray from a guiding star.

A successful salesperson knows that asking their prospect key questions is essential to pressing that prospect's hot buttons, and getting that prospect exactly what they want. Whatever the prospect likes is what the successful salesperson has to give, and even more.

The successful salesperson knows that if everything in life were free that most people would accept their offer without hesitation. Therefore, that salesperson keeps a keen eye on how they should introduce price to their prospect. They will strive to leave room for negotiation on at least three occasions, for the mere fact that most prospects will not give up without a fight. (Life is a game with no game show host.)

A successful salesperson knows that most people who buy will buy on impulse. That salesperson will thus emit an aura of urgency in their presentation. *Today* and *now* is always the best time for the prospect to buy, or else lose out forever. A prospect who has had time to think is the last thing the successful salesperson wants to hear.

And so, a successful salesperson is only as successful as his or her expectations and goals are. Their success is measured by the degree of their faith. Their ambition is their guide. Their desire propels them. And their determination guarantees their success.

These are, in summary, the thoughts that occupy the mind of the successful salesperson.

# C O N C L U S I O N

*A good symbol is the best argument, and is a missionary to persuade thousands.*
  *- Ralph Waldo Emerson*

If you have studied – as opposed to read – this book, then you have already achieved the bronze stamp of approval. If you have practiced this book, then you have achieved the silver stamp of approval. If you have gone beyond this book to a higher level of self-improvement, then you have achieved the well-envied gold stamp of approval.

Now, after studying this book you should feel confident about selling. You can officially call yourself a professional salesperson as long as you're abiding by the majority of the techniques described in this book. Think positively, be and believe in yourself, and you will do just fine.

I am a researcher who provides all the information he can about the method of selling, and who improves everyday by practicing these methods himself. My core focus on selling is to believe in myself, and stay positive with affirmations such as, "I'm good at selling." Once I'm in those modes, I stamp my own self with the seal of approval.

But you can be assured that anytime you run into problems or discouragements that this book will be by your side, to guide you along the way; to pick you back up when you fall, and to restore you whole when you begin to feel incomplete. You have a marvelous resource that many other salespeople wish to discover.

Whether you are a beginner or a long time pro at Sales, you will benefit strongly by opening up this book to refresh what has become stale for you, or to "discover" what you once did not know. You can discover new things you've missed even after studying this book for the thousandth time. Sales is a vast ocean, and you are but an octopus swimming it – grasping all the information you can with your tentacles.

Good luck and best wishes are yours on your road to success. I desire to see your name stamped with the golden seal of approval.

# Glossary

---

## CERTAIN WORDS MUST BE DEFINED

These definitions have been tailored to suit this book. They do not cover all the words you will find in sales, but they do give you a preview of some of the most common words that you will come across in the profession of selling.

**Achievement:**   The results of your effort to succeed

**Act:**   To do, rather than just think or talk about

**Acting:**   Extending one's enthusiasm to match the prospect's interest

**Ambition:**   The degree of how much one wants to succeed

**Anchoring:**   Resurfacing pleasant memories through tactical methods

**Aura:**   The invisible energy that radiates from the body

**Belief In Self:**   The knowledge that you can get what you want done

**Benefit:**   The usefulness of something or someone to another

**Benefit Statement:** A clear statement of why the prospect should buy from you

**Binding:**   Two or more things or ideas put together to create options

**Body Language:** A non-verbal form of communication that can influence others

**Change:**   The process of seeing things a different way through awareness

**Close Ended:**   In reference to questions: questions that involve a *yes* or *no* answer

**Command:**   A powerful suggestion aimed at the prospect's subconscious mind

**Competition:**   Others, fighting for first place to sell their version of what you sell

**Compliment:**   A statement intended to make someone feel good within

**Common Ground:** Things you share in common with another person

**Confidence:**   The belief that you will ultimately succeed no matter what

**Conscious mind:** One's outer, changing thoughts

**Control:** A presentation being lead by you rather than the prospect

**Conversation:** Exchange of thoughts and ideas between two or more people

**Convince:** The ability to change someone's mind

**Decision Maker:** The person who makes the final decision on buying your product

**Demand:** The degree of need for your product or service to the public

**Demonstrate:** To show, rather than just talk about

**Desire:** The degree of how much you want to do something

**Determination:** The strongest energy force used to get something accomplished

**Ease:** To put down one's defenses

**Empathy:** To sense what another person is experiencing or feeling

**Engage:** To bring someone into a conversation with you

**Enjoy:** To have a liking for someone or something

**Enthusiasm:** The method used to transfer a lively feeling

**Envision:** To mentally see something the way you would want it to be

**Fear (1):** The opposite of love

**Fear (2):** Anticipation of danger or loss

**Focus:** The art of using all one's senses for one thing at a given time

**Goal:** The number, time or thing that you have set to succeed in

**Good Luck:** Another word for positive thinking, or positive energy

**Highball:** A high price given that can be negotiated downwards

**Hot Buttons:** Things the prospect likes, that gets them excited

**Humor:** Any method used to lighten up the mood

**Hypnosis:** A procedure of tapping into a prospect's subconscious mind

**Hypnotic Techniques:** Command cues toward the prospect's subconscious mind

**Impulse:** To act quickly based on feelings rather than reasoning

**Influence:** To have an effective change on someone mentally

**Like:** To appreciate a certain quality in someone or something

**Love:** The desire to know and experience

**Marketing:** Any organized system involved in creating and increasing attention and interest to something.

**Mirror & Match:** Acting the same way your prospect does. See Pacing

**Motivation:** The reason that inspires us to do what we do

**Need:** A condition in which the prospect lacks something

**Negative Thinking:** Not putting out the effort to look at the bright side of things

**Negotiate:** To come to a reasonable agreement that benefits all

**Objection:** Excuses prospects make

**Open-ended:** In questions: questions that need more than a *yes* or no answer

**Opinion:** A choice someone sticks with based on feelings

**Qualify:** An interview to determine if a prospect's needs/wants can be met

**Pacing:** Purposely acting like the prospect, without mocking them. See Mirror Match

**Pain:** The pressure that increases pleasure when success is achieved

**Pause:** To emphasize a point by being silent for a second or two afterwards

**Perception:** The way a person sees people, things or ideas through their own eyes

**Persistency:** The act of not giving up in spite of much resistance

**Persuasion:** The ability to get someone to act upon a convincing argument

**Pleasure:** A desirable, good feeling

**Positive Thinking:** A choice between two ways of thinking – the other one being negative

**Power Questions:** Particular questions that can help in persuading others

**Power Words:** Particular words that can help in persuading others

**Preview:** A sneak peek summary of your presentation

**Promise:** A guarantee that your word will be fulfilled

**Prospect:** A potential customer

**Prospecting:** The search for applicable prospects wherever you can

**Prove:** To show or demonstrate as evidence.

**Rapport:**            A relationship built or a kinship developed

**Referrals:**          Prospects that your satisfied customers recommend to you

**Rejection (1):**      The rude thing that some prospects will do to you

**Rejection (2):**      The refusal of certain prospects to listen to what you have to say

**Request:**            To ask for something

**Sales:**              The method of selling. See Selling

**Satisfaction:**       The feeling that occurs after getting what one wants

**Self Doubt:**         The enemy of self belief, that holds you back from success

**Selling:**            The method of changing minds through persuasive techniques.

**Subconscious mind:** One's inner, embedded thoughts

**Tag Questions:**      Statements that are made, with an approval question at the end

**The Close:**          The method used to confirm that a sale will be or is made

**The Presentation:** The rationale or argument used to persuade the prospect

**Tie Downs:**          See Tag Questions

**Trust:**              Reasons to believe that there is genuine care and good will

**Urgency:**            A presentation that right now is the best or only time to act

**Want:**               A condition that would satisfy the prospect's desire

**Willpower:**          The degree of not wanting to give up, no matter what

# APPENDIX – RESEARCH STUDIES

The Mehrabian's Communication Study: States that persuading others with words accounts for 7%; persuading others with tone of voice accounts for 38%; and persuasion through non-verbal forms of communication, otherwise known as body language, accounts for 55%. 7% words, 38% tone of voice, 55% body language

❖

The University of Chicago Study: States that a person's pupil will dilate (expand) when they are experiencing something pleasant or pleasurable. For instance if someone likes you, their pupil will most likely dilate. If they don't, it will constrict.

❖

Studies show that smiling helps to release endorphins (pain blockers), that make us feel better and/or serotonins (happy hormones) that relax us and improve our mood.

# INDEX

**229**

**231**

**233**

www.ingramcontent.com/pod-product-compliance
Lightning Source LLC
Chambersburg PA
CBHW060008210326
41520CB00009B/857